INDIA-UZBEKISTAN PARTNERSHIP IN REGIONAL PEACE AND STABILITY: CHALLENGES AND PROSPECTS

INDIA-UZBEKISTAN PARTNERSHIP IN REGIONAL PEACE AND STABILITY: CHALLENGES AND PROSPECTS

Editors

Maj Gen Rajiv Narayanan, AVSM, VSM (Retired),
Dr. Batir Tursunov, ISRS
&
Mr Gaurav Kumar

(Established 1870)

United Service Institution of India

New Delhi

Vij Books India Pvt Ltd

New Delhi (India)

Published by

Vij Books India Pvt Ltd
(Publishers, Distributors & Importers)
2/19, Ansari Road
Delhi – 110 002
Phones: 91-11-43596460, 91-11-47340674
Fax: 91-11-47340674
e-mail: vijbooks@rediffmail.com

ISBN: 978-93-88161-16-9 (Hardback)

Contents

SECTION – III

SECTION – IV

SECTION – V

Foreword

Lt Gen PK Singh, PVSM, AVSM (Retired)
Director, USI of India

India and Uzbekistan's relations are deeply rooted in ancient history. There are many references to this region in India's ancient texts; the Sakas, the rulers of this region are supposed to have participated in the epic battles of Mahabharata in India during the ancient times. The '*Uttarpath*', or the Northern Trade Route, connected India to the fabled Silk Route via Uzbekistan. The towns of Samarkand, Bukhara, Fergana emerged as major trading centres and provided India with land connectivity to China and Europe.

The colonial period, however, saw the disruption of these ancient linkages and a *Great Game* unfolded in Afghanistan between the British and the Russian Empires. After the independence of India, it maintained close interactions with the Uzbek Soviet Socialist Republic during the Soviet Union times; however the lack of connectivity was even then a severe constraint. Tashkent is entrenched in the contemporary Indian minds, being associated with the Tashkent Declaration of 1966 – the peace accord between India and Pakistan after the 1965 War, and the sad demise of India's then Prime Minister, Shri Lal Bahadur Shastri, on 11 Jan 1966 immediately after the accord was signed.

The descent of Afghanistan into chaos since the Soviet invasion in 1979 and the US – Pakistan counter to it, the rise of extremism under the Taliban and Al Qaeda, the US intervention post 9/11 and the emergence of many extremist factions has had a major impact on the security and the geo-strategic dynamics of Central and South Asia. The economic growth potential of both the regions, post the independence of the Central Asian nations, has been severely hampered on account of this factor. An additional constraint has been the strained relations between USA and Iran ever since the overthrow of the Shah of Iran. Of late this relationship has turned very acrimonious with the USA unilaterally walking out of the Nuclear Deal that was reached on 02 April 2015 between the P5 of UN plus Germany and Iran.

Within Central Asia, Uzbekistan occupies a central location sharing borders with the other four nations and providing connectivity to Central Asia with both Afghanistan and Iran – veritably the *Heart of Central Asia*. After years of intra-regional disregard President Shavkat Mirziyoyev's outreach in the region has had a positive impact on the inter-state relations. It also provides an impetus to India's '*Connect Central Asia Policy*', as enunciated in Jun 2012. This augurs well for the stability, security and development of the larger neighbourhood encompassing, Central and South Asia, Afghanistan and Iran.

The current geo-strategic flux that has created strategic uncertainties, however also throws up opportunities for both India and Uzbekistan to work together for regional peace and stability. This book is thus a timely effort by scholars and experts form the United Service Institution (USI) of India and the Institute for Strategic and Regional Studies (ISRS), under the President of Uzbekistan, in this regard. It would provide a good foundation for the other neighbouring countries to jointly overcome such challenges.

Foreword

Dr. Vladimir Norov

Director, ISRS under the President of the Republic of Uzbekistan

For millennia, close cultural and civilisational ties united Uzbekistan and India. Despite the various vicissitudes and difficult periods in history, as well as the relative geographical distance from each other, the peoples of our countries have maintained special friendly relations based on the commonality and similarity of unique cultures, centuries-old traditions, sustainable spiritual value and world view orientations.

Moreover, Uzbekistan and India are united by the fact that both countries have entered a qualitatively new period of their comprehensive development and demonstrate high rates of economic growth. Such dynamic processes in these states become system factors that will largely determine the trajectory of deep structural changes in Central and South Asia, respectively.

On the other hand, Uzbekistan and India are pursuing an active, open and peaceful foreign policy aimed at strengthening stability in Central and South Asia and the world at large. Surely, strategic prospects of not only Uzbek-Indian relations, but also the future of cooperation between the two key regions of the vast Eurasian space, are directly related to solution of urgent problems of regional security.

All of the above, without any exaggeration, allows us today, in the era of ambiguous processes of globalisation and transformation of the modern world order, to look with great optimism in the future of Uzbek-Indian relations. It is this idea that is the quintessence of our joint research project "India-Uzbekistan partnership in regional peace and stability: challenges and prospects".

Leading specialists of the Institute for Strategic and Regional Studies under the President of the Republic of Uzbekistan and the United Service Institution of India have taken part in the preparation of this book. In their analytical articles, the authors have presented their own vision of the past, present and future of Uzbek-Indian relations in the face of the persistent acute problems of regional security in Central Asia and Afghanistan.

In my opinion, an attempt of joint intellectual reflection on the urgent issues of regional security and development in Central Asia, directly or indirectly affecting the interests of Uzbekistan and India, is more relevant and timely than ever. What is it caused by?

First, active regional diplomacy of the Indian government can give a new dynamism to India's "Connect Central Asia Policy". In 2016 Prime Minister Narendra Modi visited all countries of the region, which became a landmark event in the newest history of the Indian-Central Asian relations. Moreover, full membership in the Shanghai Cooperation Organisation opens strategic opportunities for India to enhance the effectiveness of bilateral and multilateral cooperation with the countries of Central Asia.

Second, the "new political reality" in Central Asia, which became possible due to the active regional policy of the President Shavkat Mirziyoyev. Deep positive changes in the interstate relations of the Central Asian countries, achieved in an unprecedentedly short period of time, have created favorable conditions for the progressive development of not only intra-regional cooperation, but also the intensification of their interaction with international partners, including India.

Third, the established personal warm relationship between the President of Uzbekistan Sh. Mirziyoyev and the Prime Minister of India Narendra Modi. The leaders of the two states have already held a number of productive meetings, which revealed common positive attitude of the parties to every possible strengthening of the multifaceted cooperation in the spheres of trade and economy, investment and high technologies, energy and transport, culture and tourism.

In this context, I would like to express my conviction that this book will let us take a fresh look and assess the huge but not yet revealed potential of Uzbek-Indian relations, as well as identify their long-term prospects and strategic importance for strengthening security and sustainable development in Central and South Asia. Obviously, not only Uzbekistan and India will benefit from this, but also neighboring countries, which are now showing a growing desire to jointly overcome modern challenges and threats in order to ensure security and common prosperity in this vast region.

Abbreviations

AML	-	Anti-money Laundering
ANSF	-	Afghan National Security Force
ANASTU	-	Afghan National Agriculture Sciences and Technology University
APAPPS	-	Afghanistan- Pakistan Action Plan for Peace and Solidarity
BRICS	-	Brazil, Russia, India, China, South Africa
CARs	-	Central Asian Republics
CCAP	-	Connect Central Asia Policy
CPEC	-	China Pakistan Economic Corridor
CFT	-	Combating the Financing of Terrorism
CIS	-	Commonwealth of Independent States
CTITF	-	Counter-Terrorism Implementation Task Force
DoD	-	Department of Defence
EAG	-	Eurasia Group
EBRD	-	European Bank for Reconstruction and Development
ETIM	-	East Turkestan Islamic Movement
GCTS	-	Global Counter Terrorism Strategy
IEC	-	Independent Election Commission
IISF	-	India International Science Festival

INSTC	-	International North South Transit Corridor
ISKP	-	Islamic State of Khorasan Province
ISRS	-	Institute for Strategic and Regional Studies, Uzbekistan
JPA	-	Joint Plan of Action
JeM	-	Jaish-e-Mohammed
LeT	-	Lashkar-e-Taiba
NATO	-	North Atlantic Treaty Organisation
OCHA	-	UN Office for Coordination of Humanitarian Affairs
OIC	-	Organisation of Islamic Cooperation
QCG	-	Quadrilateral Coordination Group
RATS	-	Regional Anti-Terrorism Structure
REO	-	Religious Extremist Organisations
SCO	-	Shanghai Cooperation Organisation
SIGAR	-	Special Inspector General for Afghanistan Reconstruction
SPA	-	Strategic Partnership Agreement
STREET	-	Strategy to Reach, Empower and Educate Teenagers
TAPI	-	Turkmenistan–Afghanistan–Pakistan–India Pipeline
UN	-	United Nations
UNODC	-	United Nations Office on Drugs and Crime
UNGA	-	United Nations General Assembly
USI	-	United Service Institution of India, India

Introduction

Major General Rajiv Narayanan

Kamboja, Parama-Kamboja, Sakas, Kushan are some of the ancient Mahajanpads and kingdoms that have linked India and Uzbekistan from the times of yore. Trade via the '*Uttarpath*', or the Northern Trade Route, provided the overland links for India to China and Europe via the Ancient Silk Route. Such interactions over millennia became the conduit for cultural linkages between the two nations. Buddhism travelled from India to Central Asia and China via this route. This region has, therefore, always been of cultural and historical importance to India. These linkages continued till the British colonized South Asia and the Tsarist Russia subsumed the Central Asian region within their empire. The subsequent 'Great Game' between these two empires in Afghanistan led to the disruption of these ancient relations. The overthrow of the Tsarist Empire and the establishment of the Soviet Union shut the door of British India to this region.

Post gaining Independence from the British, India reconnected with Uzbekistan due to its good relations with the Soviet Union. Tashkent is embedded in India's memory as the place where the India – Pakistan peace accord was signed in Jan 1966 post the 1965 war. It also carries the sad memory of the untimely death of the then Indian Prime Minister, Shri Lal Bahadur Shastri, on 11 Jan 1966 immediately after signing the accord. However, the lack of direct connectivity to the region and India's bleak economic condition hampered re-establishment of the ancient trade linkages.

Since their independence from the Soviet Union in 1991, the Central Asian states have undergone path breaking transformation in nation building. The geographical advantage that accrues to Central

Asia is twofold: its geo-strategic location as a land bridge between East Asia – South Asia – West Asia and Europe, and its abundant natural resources. Uzbekistan occupies a very central location within Central Asia, having borders with the rest of the nations and providing shortest connectivity to both Afghanistan and Iran.

However, the invasion of Afghanistan by the Soviet Union in 1979 and its subsequent counter by the US in the 1980s utilizing Pakistan sponsored jihadists and Afghanistan's descent into chaos post-Soviet withdrawal in 1989 with the spread of Islamic Terrorists impacted the Central Asian states negatively. This coupled with the deteriorating relations between USA and Iran post the Iranian Revolution and the US led intervention in Afghanistan post the 9/11 event, effectively isolated the region from global connectivity, thereby inhibiting their growth. Concurrently the intra-regional growth was impacted by due to the inertia, aloofness and disregard for regional issues by the states.

The global geo-political churnings have a deep resonance in this region also, which is looked at by India as its extended neighbourhood. These churnings have led to this period of strategic uncertainties, which is witnessing new alignments that are either competing with or supplanting the old arrangements. This has caused geo-strategic and geo-political flux globally that also impacts Central and South Asia. However, with these challenges come opportunities to strengthen relations and expand sphere for new partnerships for the mutual benefit of these regions. With the aim to tap the opportunity to enhance political, economic and strategic ties, India's policy towards this region has moved towards 'Connect North'. The 'Connect Central Asia Policy' was enunciated in 2012, but the impetus has emerged now with the changing dynamics of the regions.

After years of apathy towards intra-regional trade, connectivity and better political and diplomatic relations, the initiative taken by President Shavkat Mirziyoyev to reach out to the neighbouring countries augurs well for Central Asia as also for the extended neighbourhood. However, the elephant in the room remains the instability in Afghanistan due to violent Islamic extremism, coordinated, trained, funded and sponsored from across its borders, and Pakistan's continued intransigence to providing connectivity between South and Central Asia. This is where India and Uzbekistan can jointly work towards regional peace and stability and provide a foundation to achieve the sustainable development goals, thereby providing peace and prosperity to this extended neighbourhood.

Leading experts and scholars of the Institute for Strategic and Regional Studies under the President of Uzbekistan and the United Service Institution of India have come together to prepare this book – 'India-Uzbekistan Partnership in Regional Peace and Stability: Challenges and Prospects'. The book has five Sections, each dealing with a specific topic and providing both the Uzbek and Indian perspectives, by authors from respective countries. It would be very helpful to the decision makers of both the countries to build on the convergences and work towards mitigating the divergences, if any.

Section – I looks at the 'Challenges and Prospects of Regional Security in Central Asia', and provide an insight into the issues that beset the region and the extant structures that can be strengthened to achieve sustainable security within Central Asia. **Section – II** studies the 'Role and Approach, of both India and Uzbekistan respectively, in Conflict Resolution and Peace Building in Afghanistan'. One of the keys to India's transport connectivity with Uzbekistan and rest of Central Asia is Afghanistan, the other being the Chabahar port in Iran. As such conflict resolution and peace building in Afghanistan is in the best interests of both the countries. However, the presence of global players and regional powers, each working at cross-purposes, to further respective national interests, exacerbates the situation in Afghanistan. This section would provide an insight to feasible joint efforts towards this end to the policy makers of both countries. It could also be the platform for other Central Asian nations and like-minded regional players to join this effort. **Section – III** provides an insight into the 'Prospects for Cooperation on Regional Connectivity, Trade and Transit between India and Uzbekistan'. This delves into the issues hampering connectivity and trade, and the options that are emerging due to the change in both countries' policies. It provides an insight into the opportunities that emerge and can be optimised for the benefit of both countries and the regions.

Section – IV deals with the 'Effective Management of Islamic Radicalisation of Youth' in both countries. Considering the 'Youth Bulge' in both Central and South Asia, with both ensure that this phenomenon provides them with a 'Demographic Dividend'; however, the Islamic radicalisation is a clear and present danger that has very negative portends for the extended neighbourhood as exemplified by the problems faced by Pakistan – more due to its own policy of state sponsorship for such radicalisation. India and Uzbekistan have had varied experience in dealing with this threat and these provide opportunities to both countries to build on these, thereby strengthening the fabric of the society to negate this menace. Finally, **Section – V** provides an 'Appraisal of Indo-Uzbek Relations and the Way Forward'. It sums up the extant relations and looks at ways to improve and strengthen the same.

There are many facets to the relationship between countries and between regions. This book provides an insight into a small segment of the same and would be of use to not just the policy makers but also the students interested in the geo-politics of this extended neighbourhood. It could also form the basis for further studies over an expanded scope.

SECTION – I

An Assessment of Challenges and Prospects of Regional Security in Central Asia – Uzbekistan's View

Rustam Khuramov

Structural changes are underway in the contemporary system of international relations under the influence of globalisation. Political and economic interdependence are increasing among states in an unprecedented level. In these conditions, the development of the international political situation is becoming more intensive, less manageable and unpredictable. Geopolitical struggle among great powers for spheres of influence and resources are growing, militarisation, confrontation in the cyberspace are intensifying.

The range of threats to regional security and stability, such as terrorism, religious extremism, drug trafficking, transnational crime are expanding. The problems of food, energy and environmental security are exacerbated. The growing gap between wealthy and poor countries is leading to aggravation of interethnic and confessional tensions.

In these conditions, being located in the very heart of Eurasia, with a total population of more than 70 million people Central Asia is an important link connecting Europe and the Middle East, South and East Asia. Moreover, Central Asia is one of the "youngest" regions in terms of the age composition of the population: young people make up about 60 per cent, while in the world this figure does not exceed 20 per cent.

According to experts, the situation in neighboring and distant regions, where armed confrontations have been continuing, the growing scale of challenges and threats of terrorism and religious extremism, drug trafficking and organised crime will systemically impact the stability and security of Central Asia. In this vein, the security of Central Asia is an integral part of global security. At the same time, the states of the region play a significant role in strengthening international security. The ability of the Central Asian countries in working together to ensure peace, stability and prosperity in the region will largely determine the dynamics of the most important processes in Eurasia.

Today, we may characterise the situation in Central Asia with the presence of favorable conditions for the development of multifaceted and mutually beneficial interstate cooperation between the countries of the region. High level political dialogue has noticeably been intensified; inter-regional ties of the neighboring countries have been increased. As a result, we are observing the rise in trade and economic relations, and most importantly, a new impetus given to the process of resolving long-standing region-wide problems. Scholars in the field of politics argue that the past two years (2017-2018) will be marked in history as the times of beginning of a new era in interstate relations of regional countries.

Because of the political will and active strategic actions taken by the political elites of these neighboring states, the region started showing new signs of political life. Assessing the dynamics of the latest developments in the region experts argued that the level of political confidence has significantly increased among the Central Asia countries.

Moreover, in a very short period of time absolutely "new political atmosphere" has been created in the region, which contributes to strengthening contacts in all areas and reducing the conflict potential in the region.

Revealing the essence and the content of active regional dialogue in Central Asia, Ilan Berman, the Vice President of the American Foreign Policy Council argued that the main drivers of current change taking place in the region are "the peaceful transition of power in Uzbekistan in 2016 and new large scale economic reforms launched in the country by President Shavkat Mirziyoyev. He also declared to recalibrate Tashkent's foreign policy toward the neighboring countries"[1].

During his inaugural speech, President Mirziyoyev gave a strong signal on his readiness to take a new approach toward regional issues, saying his commitment to "an open, friendly, and pragmatic position" towards the Central Asian states. Uzbekistan, bordering with all the countries of the region is interested in turning the space into a zone of stability, sustainable development and good-neighborliness.

In 2017, by the initiative of President Mirziyoyev and following the results of the nationwide discussion, Uzbekistan for the first time in history adopted the Strategy of Actions on the five priority directions of development in 2017-2021, where the main tasks of modernising public administration, democratising society, ensuring the rule of law, liberalisation of the economy, strengthening the social protection of the population, and conducting active and initiative foreign policy are identified.

Special attention in the Strategy is paid to strengthening the independence and sovereignty of the state, increasing the role of the country as a full-fledged member of international relations, creating a belt of security, stability and prosperity around Uzbekistan. In this regard, Helena Fraser, UN Resident Coordinator in Uzbekistan, noted that the Strategy and the new foreign policy approach implemented on its basis on strengthening ties with neighboring countries is the guarantee of future prosperity and stable development of not only Uzbekistan, but also of all the Central Asia.

In his Address to the UN's General Assembly in September, 2017 Shavkat Mirziyoyev, describing the core directions of Uzbekistan's modern foreign policy, once again confirmed that the region of Central Asia is a main priority and named it to be "a conscious choice". He stated that, "a peaceful and economically

---

1   Foreign Affairs, August 8, 2017 "Central Asia's Encouraging Development" Ilan Berman https://www.foreignaffairs.com/articles/central-asia/2017-08-08/central-asias-encouraging-development

prosperous Central Asia is our most important goal and key task".

Moreover, emphasising the intensification of interstate contacts, he initiated organising the summit of heads of the Central Asian states. As he mentioned, "holding the regular consultation meetings" of the presidents would promote consolidation of the trend towards rapprochement with neighbors. In response to this, the leaders of other countries of the region have demonstrated their readiness and sincere desire for cooperation, as well as their responsibility for a common future.

In this vein, international analysts argue that, achieving the long-term stability and sustainable development in Central Asia depends on the strengthening of mutual trust among the states of the region, development of international transport corridors, economic diversification, rational approaches to the use of trans-boundary water recourses and completing delimitation and demarcation of state borders.

In this regard most importantly, the process of resolving long-standing region-wide problems has received a new impetus. It has been achieved positive progresses in the issue of delimitation and demarcation of state borders among the countries of the region. In this issue, Uzbekistan signed agreements on the state borders with Kazakhstan and Turkmenistan. Tashkent and Bishkek agreed the demarcation and delimitation of 85 percent of their borders. Yaroslav Trofimov, Wall Street Journal analyst concluded that, this was huge milestone because only a few years ago there had been clashes between Uzbek and Kyrgyz border guards.[2]

Bilateral relations between Uzbekistan and Tajikistan started with a new page after the state visit of President Mirziyoyev to Dushanbe in March 2018. Edward Lemon, expert on Central Asian affairs argued that the resumption of transport air links and easing of visa regulations would certainly improve the lives of border

---

2 Wall Street Journal Oct. 5, 2017. "Long-Feuding Central Asia Nations Move to Reconcile" YaroslavTrofimov https://www.wsj.com/articles/long-feuding-central-asia-nations-move-to-reconcile-1507195800

communities, and benefit Tajikistan's economy in particular.[3]

Sachary Witlin, an analyst for the Eurasia Group in Washington, argued that "few could have expected Mirziyoyev to so quickly revive Uzbekistan's foreign relations with the rest of Central Asia and beyond and to do it so quickly raises hopes for political reforms"[4].

Moreover according to foreign experts, "these developments and others suggest a degree of political consolidation and innovation that was unthinkable even ten years ago". The head of the UN Regional Centre for Preventive Diplomacy in Central Asia Petko Draganov in his speech at the conference, which was held in August 2017 in Tashkent titled "Central Asia – the main priority of Uzbekistan's foreign policy" underlined that all the initiatives of the Uzbek leadership aimed at bringing all the countries of Central Asia for common development and progress are fully conformable to the fundamental purposes and goals of the UN.

Catherine Putz, analyst on Central Asian issues at "The Diplomat", wrote that repairing bilateral relationships is just one piece of this puzzle; a second is Tashkent's emerging embrace of multilateral cooperation.[5]

In accordance to it in November 2017, the ancient city of Uzbekistan, Samarkand hosted an international conference on Security and Sustainable Development in Central Asia under the auspices of United Nations. Agenda of the forum titled "Central Asia: Shared Past and a Common Future, Cooperation for Sustainable Development and Mutual Prosperity". During the

---

3   The Central Asian and Caucuses Analyst, October 19, 2016. "Signs of improving relations between Uzbekistan and Tajikistan but tensions remain", Edward Lemon https://cacianalyst.org/publications/analytical-articles/item/13405-sings-of-improving-relations-between-uzbekistan-and-tajikistan-but-tensions-remain.html

4   Forbes, September14, 2017. "Eurasia's Latest Economic Reboot Can Be Found In Uzbekistan", Kenneth Raposa https://www.forbes.com/sites/kenraposa/2017/09/14/eurasias-new-perestroika-uzbekistan-silk-road-china/#7a9c38c86f25

5   Ibidem 2.

conference, experts discussed the issues of strengthening peace and stability in Central Asia, development of regional cooperation, as well as contribution of international structures, primarily UN, to the implementation of sustainable development projects. At the end of the conference, it adopted a joint communiqué calling on the UN General Assembly to adopt a resolution on ensuring peace, security and sustainable development in Central Asia.

The conference was attended by ministers of foreign affairs of all states of Central Asia, heads of such authoritative organisations, as the United Nations, the European Union, the OSCE, the SCO, the CIS, the EBRD, representatives of diplomatic corps, distinguished experts, and media – more than 500 participants.

At the conference, President Mirziyoyev stressed that the first results achieved should not be a reason for complacency. We are still "at the beginning of the road". He underlined that Uzbekistan is strongly convinced that the main goal for the coming years should be the agreement in approaches to transform Central Asia into a territory of peace, good-neighborliness and prosperity. According to him, the region faces the most important tasks - jointly eliminating conditions and causes that fuel and provoke the conflict potential, ensure matching of national development prospects with the region-wide priorities.

In this regard, it is important to outline the positions and approaches of the Republic of Uzbekistan on the further enhancement of cooperation and providing sustainable development in Central Asia.

First, the further development of trade and economic ties, and creation of favorable conditions for the growth of mutual trade in the region. In 2017, trade turnover between Uzbekistan and the countries of the region increased by an average of 20 per cent, and with individual states - by almost 70 percent. In the first half of 2018 trade had been increased by 50 per cent.

According to the calculations of the United Nations, effective cooperation of the Central Asian countries in following 10 years could double the regional trade. A practical contribution to this task could be the creation of a Regional Economic Forum and the establishment of the Association of Heads of Regions of the Central Asian states. This will allow for a direct dialogue between the business communities and strengthen inter-regional ties.

Secondly, the use of the transit and logistics potential of the region more efficiently and ensure the faster development of the transport and communication infrastructure. Today, the states of the region are trying to use their advantageous geographical position not only to enter the world markets, but also to act as one of the links of the transcontinental transport communication. In particular, since early 2017, a high-speed railway between Uzbekistan and Kazakhstan has been launched.

Turkmenistan and Uzbekistan opened new railway and automobile bridges connecting Turkmenabad-Farab over the Amu Darya, which has become an important part of the transport-transit route "Uzbekistan-Turkmenistan-Iran-Oman". Further, an agreement was also reached on the start of the construction of the railway line connecting "Uzbekistan-Kyrgyzstan-China", and for its initial survey.

Thirdly, further strengthening and intensifying cooperation among the Central Asian countries on identifying and preventing terrorist cross-border activities, defeating the recruitment channels for militants, fighting against financing terrorism, arms smuggling, illegal migration and drug trafficking. Countering these challenges and threats would only be effective in the framework of bilateral and multilateral cooperation mechanisms. President Mirziyoyev emphasised that it is necessary to abandon division of "ours and others" threats and continue to adhere to the principle of "indivisibility of security".

Fourthly, continuing the regional efforts in the integration of Afghanistan to the regional trade-economic, transport-communication and energy links. The early achievement of peace in Afghanistan is crucial to ensuring security and stability in the region, which is in the fundamental interest of Central Asian countries. This will open new strategic opportunity for fully realising the potential of trade and economic cooperation, implementing projects in the field of transport communications.

Significant contribution to the overall efforts directed to stabilising the situation in Afghanistan will undoubtedly contribute to the Kabul's active involvement in the processes of regional cooperation in Central Asia.

Fifth, completing the process of delimitation and demarcation of state borders, strengthening the confidence building measures by taking into account mutual interests on the basis of reasonable compromises and complementing exchange.

Sixth, the key direction of interstate relations in the region remains the strengthening of cultural and humanitarian contacts, ties of friendship and good-neighborliness between our states and peoples.

In this regard, it should be noted that in March 2018, the first consultative meeting of the heads of Central Asian states was held in Astana by the initiative of the President of Uzbekistan. It was to maintain a regular confidential dialogue and develop a coordinated approach on topical regional issues.

It bears to emphasise that this structure is not about creating a new international organisation in Central Asia or any integrated structure with its charter and supranational bodies. This will be aimed exclusively at discussing key issues for regional development.

On June 22, 2018, the UN General Assembly adopted a resolution on "Strengthening regional and international cooperation for ensuring peace, stability and sustainable development in the Central Asian region". According to the Ministry of Foreign Affairs of Uzbekistan, the document, the draft for which was developed by Uzbekistan jointly with the neighboring states of Central Asia, was unanimously supported by all UN member states.

The adoption of the resolution was the culmination of the initiative of the President of the Republic of Uzbekistan Shavkat

Mirziyoyev, put forward during the 72nd session of the UN General Assembly in September 2017. The resolution recognises the important role of Central Asian countries in ensuring peace, stability and sustainable development in the region, as well as in promoting regional and international cooperation. Introducing the draft text, the representative of Uzbekistan said that its main purpose was to gain the support of the international community in the efforts of Central Asian States to foster closer collaborations in order to ensure peace and stability in the region. He also emphasised their shared spiritual and cultural heritage. The Assembly expressed its support for the ongoing regional efforts to strengthen economic cooperation and stability in Central Asia, and encouraged their efforts to promote peace and development in Afghanistan.

The resolution emphasised the importance of developing and strengthening bilateral and regional cooperation in the sphere of rational and integrated use of water and energy resources in Central Asia. It called upon UN Member States to support the Central Asian nations in their efforts to mitigate the consequences of the drying up of the Aral Sea.[6]

Noting with satisfaction the regional support for the initiative of Uzbekistan to convene the Consultative Meetings of the leaders of the Central Asian states on regular basis, the resolution underlined the need to effectively use the platform of such consultations to jointly address the pressing problems of the region. The document welcomes holding of the first summit of the heads of Central Asia states on March 15, 2018 in Astana.

A new level of political confidence in the region gave a powerful impetus to the development of institutions of public diplomacy, cultural ties, and expanding contacts between bordering provinces, parliamentarians, public organisations and citizens. In this sense, experts argue that, Central Asia's ills (its economic ills, at least), could be cured by greater regional cooperation.[7]

---

6   https://www.un.org/press/en/2018/ga12030.doc.htm

7   Diplomat, September 30, 2017. "Uzbekistan in the Spotlight-The centre of Central Asia has turned its focus to multilateral regional cooperation",

American expert Ilan Berman underscored that, "nearby states are taking notice, and there is growing approval in capitals around the region of this new good-neighbor policy". These dramatic changes have helped to create a strong and reliable foundation for regional cooperation in Central Asia. Nevertheless, there are some key trends and challenges that will have a direct impact on the regional security and sustainable development in Central Asia.

First, growing geopolitical confrontation and escalating tensions in a number of key regions of the world would have its effects on this newly emerging regional security architecture in Central Asia. In these conditions, the fundamental condition for ensuring regional security will be preservation of the geopolitical balance and pluralism in Central Asia.

Secondly, one of the major sources of threat to regional and international security remains the ongoing war in Afghanistan. Unfortunately, the current military and political situation in the country is largely uncertain and difficult to predict. This trend, especially in the backdrop of events in the Middle East, causes the concern in the world community in the context of actualisation of challenges and threats of extremism, terrorism and drug trafficking that affect the stability and security of not only Central Asia but also other regions of the world.

At the 71st session of the UN General Assembly, Abdulaziz Kamilov, Foreign Minister of Uzbekistan stressed that Afghan conflict could be settled only on basis of intra-Afghan national accord and through peaceful political negotiations under auspices of the United Nations and without any preliminary conditions.

Such instability and terrorism has a major impact not only for the countries of Central Asia, but also in neighboring South Asia. Today, no one doubts that the problem of the indivisibility of security assumes special significance for developing common approaches and adequate responses to the challenges and threats to regional and global security. The actualisation of this problem is evidenced by the phenomenon of the "Islamic state", whose ranks are filled by not

Catherine Putz https://thediplomat.com/2017/09/uzbekistan-in-the-spotlight/

only citizens of Asian states, but also by immigrants from the EU countries.

Complex negative trends in the global financial and economic system also impacts the solution of priority tasks for ensuring sustainable development of Central Asian countries. The preservation of high growth rates of national economies and the progressive improvement of the welfare of the population of the countries depends on many constraints. The lack of a reliable transport and communication corridor, ensuring a stable access of the Central Asian countries to the large markets in Europe and Asia hampers their full integration into the global trade. This increases their vulnerability to external challenges and threats.

One-sided development of the economies (resource based) of most countries of the region strongly binds them to the vagaries of the world commodity market, which limits their efforts in modernising and diversifying their economies. A diversified structure of the economy is an essential necessity of not only sustainable development, but also for social and political stability. One that is a major cause for concern is that the youth forms up to 60 per cent of the population of the Central Asia. This constrains the Central Asian governments to have much better employment policy, requiring creation of jobs for the young generation.

The importance of this issue becomes obvious if one looks at the origins of economic turbulence in North Africa and Middle East states, where the national economies are resource dependent and solely depend on oil and gas exports.

This underlines the fact that diversified economy is not only an economic imperative, but also a geopolitical necessity to strengthen the sovereignty of the Central Asian states, and their internal immunity to external challenges and threats, including radicalisation, religious extremism and international terrorism.

In this regard, addressing the vital issues for regional development from border security to effective intra-regional multimodal transport routes is the key for sustainable development of the region. The states of the region have identified that only with the strengthening of bilateral and multilateral ties within the region, can the economic and political goals be achieved. So far, they tested the colorful contacts with different actors, without paying enough attention to regional cooperation, but today economically prosperous, secure Central Asia is an absolute imperative for all the countries of the region. Any major regional projects in the spheres of transport, communication and energy cannot be realised without active interaction of the regional states and without ensuring a high level of cooperation and political confidence.

An Assessment of Challenges and Prospects of Regional Security in Central Asia: An Indian Perspective

Ambassador Asoke Kumar Mukerji

Introduction

Located in the heart of the Asian landmass, the five independent states of Central Asia (Kazakhstan, Kyrgyzstan, Tajikistan, Turkmenistan and Uzbekistan) emerged on the international stage following the dissolution of the Union of Soviet Socialist Republics (USSR) in December 1991. Since then, they have taken different approaches to developing as modern nation states. However, the regional security challenges these five independent states of Central Asia face are similar.

It is widely accepted today among strategic analysts that the four major threats to regional security in Central Asia are terrorism, religious extremism, transnational crime and drug trafficking. Any discussion of the challenges and prospects for regional security in Central Asia from an Indian perspective would need to begin by placing these security challenges to Central Asia in context.

Historical background

In the 19th century, the regional security of contemporary Central Asia was linked to the imperial interests of the Tsarist Russian and British Empires. There were two consequences of this dynamic. First, the creation of a buffer space between Tsarist Central Asia and British India through the consolidation of the Afghan state, and specifically the demarcation by 1893 of both sides of Afghanistan's Wakhan Corridor to physically separate the two empires. Above the Wakhan corridor was Russian Turkestan, while below it was the Gilgit-Baltistan region belonging to the Indian Princely State of Jammu and Kashmir, which was under British suzerainty.[1] Second, the jostling for influence over Afghanistan, directly related to the focus on regional security in the region by both the Tsarist Russian and British Empires. In this process, the Second Afghan War of 1878 played a major role in consolidating British interests.

Looked at from this perspective, today's Central Asia was not part of the political upheaval underway against the British Empire in South Asia until the First World War. During the war, the Central Powers led by Germany and Ottoman Turkey attempted to displace British influence in Afghanistan. This included support extended to Indian revolutionaries from British India in Afghanistan. They were encouraged to set up a "provisional government of India" in Kabul in December 1915 led by Raja Mahendra Pratap,[2] which lasted till 1919.

The first time the territory of Central Asia itself (which had come under Bolshevik rule following the overthrow of Tsarist Russia in 1917) featured in British imperial threat perceptions was with the establishment of the Communist Party of India in Tashkent (Uzbekistan) on 17 October 1920, followed by the setting up of an Indian Military Training School in Tashkent which functioned from October 1920 till the end of May 1921.[3] The participation of some of the alumni from the Military Training School in violent actions against British Indian rule in India catalysed British security policy towards Soviet Central Asia.

The primary aim of this policy was to continue to isolate Central Asia from India. The British objective was aided by the imposition of authoritarian Bolshevik rule in Central Asia following

---

1 'A Few Salient Points' by Frank Jacobs, *The New York Times*, December 5, 2011. Available at https://opinionator.blogs.nytimes.com/2011/12/05/a-few-salient-points/

2 "Sedition Committee Report, 1918", Government Printing Press, Calcutta, 1918, pp. 177-179.

3 "Formation of the Communist Party of India at Tashkent (1920)", available at https://cpim.org/history/formation-communist-party-india-tashkent-1920

the resolutions on "Turkestan matters" adopted on 29 June 1920 by the Politburo of the Central Committee of the Bolshevik Russian Communist Party. The decision to demarcate the existing borders of Soviet Central Asian Republics was implemented between 1924 and 1936, following which international contact between Central Asia and India was channelised through the Communist Party of the Soviet Union in Moscow.[4]

India's independence in August 1947, followed by the military annexation of Jammu and Kashmir's Gilgit-Baltistan province by Pakistan in October 1947, took away India's territorial contiguity with the Wakhan Corridor. The consolidation of friendly relations between independent India and the USSR that followed India's independence kept Soviet Central Asia as a benign part of India's security calculus, dependent on Soviet rule in the region to contain any security threats to India. This perspective changed drastically once the USSR was dissolved in December 1991, and the new independent states of Central Asia established direct state-to-state relations with India from 1992. For appreciating the new dynamics in security cooperation between India and Central Asia today, it is useful to look at the current profile of Central Asia from an Indian perspective.

A profile of Central Asia

The total population of the five Central Asian states today is 72 million. Like India, the population has a young demographic profile, the average age being 26 years. About 40 per cent of the population lives in urban areas. Kazakhstan has the largest territory of 2.7 million sq. km., and a population of 18 million; Uzbekistan, which has an area of 447,400 sq. km., has a population of 31 million; Turkmenistan has an area of 488,100 sq. km. and a population of 5.6 million; Tajikistan has an area of 142,550 sq. km. and a population of 8.7 million; and Kyrgyzstan an area of 199,950 sq.km, and a population of 5.9 million.

---

4   For a full discussion of these matters, see "Establishment of Soviet Power in Central Asia (1917-1924) by R.Y. Radjapova, Chapter 6, pp. 149-179 in The History of Civilisations of Central Asia, Volume VI, published by UNESCO, 2005.

In comparison with Central Asia's total land area of 4 million sq. km, the total land area of India is 3.28 million sq. km.[5]

Regional security challenges in Central Asia impact on the immense diversity of the populations in each of the five independent states. Diversity of population is a factor shared by Central Asia and India. From the perspective of security challenges as seen from India, the focus is on population linkages across the borders to the southern and eastern regions adjoining Central Asia, viz. Afghanistan and the Xinjiang region of China. Both these bordering regions of Central Asia are themselves targets of terrorism and religious extremism, and one of them (Afghanistan) is a major source of drugs trafficked across the world. The presence of significant Central Asian ethnic populations (Tajiks, Uzbeks and Turkmen) in the northern half of Afghanistan, as well as the presence of Uighurs from Xinjiang in Central Asia, adds to the complexity of these challenges, as kinship linkages often play a significant role in transporting security threats across the region.[6]

The fact that all the five states, which are land-locked, have invested in creating or supporting regional connectivity infrastructures increases the importance of securing these infrastructures from becoming targets of conduits of security threats. This perception was true of the ancient Silk Road and is equally true of the new Silk Route of the 21st century. India's own experience in constructing connectivity infrastructure along her land borders in the north and east takes into account the challenges of securing such infrastructure from the activity of terrorist and insurgent groups aided by external powers. This provides a good area for mutual exchanges of experience between India and Central Asia when cooperating on regional security issues.

---

5 Census of India 2001. Available at http://www.censusindia.gov.in/Census_ Data_2001/India_at_Glance/area.aspx

6 Kazakhstan shares land borders with the Russian Federation, China, Kyrgyzstan, Uzbekistan and Turkmenistan. Uzbekistan shares land borders with Kazakhstan, Kyrgyzstan, Tajikistan, Turkmenistan and Afghanistan. Turkmenistan shares land borders with Iran, Afghanistan, Uzbekistan and Kazakhstan. Tajikistan shares land borders with Uzbekistan, Kyrgyzstan, China and Afghanistan. Kyrgyzstan shares land borders with Uzbekistan, Kazakhstan, Tajikistan and China.

India and Central Asia are members of both the Shanghai Cooperation Organisation (SCO) and United Nations (UN), which have in recent years drawn up extensive programmes for cooperation in addressing challenges to Central Asian regional security. This is an area where India can contribute more pro-actively to meeting the challenges to Central Asian regional security, especially when these challenges are linked to India's own threat perceptions.

Countering Terrorism and Religious Extremism

Foremost among these common threat perceptions is the threat posed by terrorism and religious extremism. If British India was apprehensive about the ideological threat of Bolshevism from Central Asia, then independent India is apprehensive about the ideology of terrorism emanating from the Af-Pak region on Central Asia and India. This terrorist threat has its roots in the impact of the Afghan "*jihad*" against the USSR, sponsored by the United States and Saudi Arabia (and implemented through Pakistan).[7]

Indian perspectives on the origins of the threats posed by terrorism and religious extremism to the security of Central Asia factor in the decision of the five independent states to maintain their modern political structures, based on a presidential form of government, even while acknowledging their Islamic heritage. This enabled all the Central Asian states to become members of the Organisation of Islamic Cooperation[8], although none of them decided to rename their states as "Islamic Republics". External elements adhering to the Wahabi school of Islam have sought to influence the outcome of the evolution of Central Asia through their perspectives on what the region's Islamic heritage meant, and the role of Islam in nation-building. This has often conflicted with Central Asia's broader movement focusing on stable, modern, pluralistic societies aspiring for socio-economic development. Such conflicts became

---

7 "Charlie Wilson's War" by George Crille, 9 November 2003. Available on C-Span at https://www.c-span.org/video/?179144-10/charlie-wilsons-war

8 While Kyrgyzstan, Tajikistan and Turkmenistan joined the OIC in 1992, Kasakhstan and Uzbekistan joined the organisation in 1995.

the crucible for terrorism to take root in contemporary Central Asia, especially in the densely populated Ferghana valley that is shared by Uzbekistan, Kyrgyzstan and Tajikistan.

The population of Tajikistan, which neighbours Afghanistan (with its own significant Tajik population), was directly impacted by the 'descent into chaos' of the 1990s. This was marked by the coming to power of the Taliban in Afghanistan, supported by Pakistan.[9] Terrorism unleashed a bloody civil war in Tajikistan, which was eventually ended by a Russian-brokered truce in 1997.[10]

The proponents of using violent extremism and terrorism in Central Asia draw upon the historical memories of the Basmachi rebellion against Russian Tsarist and Bolshevik rule in Central Asia during 1916-1926. In their narrative, support for the Afghan Mujahedeen's fight against the "godless Communism" of the Soviet Union must now be seamlessly transferred to violently destabilizing post-Bolshevik governments, in the region sometimes referred to as Turkestan.[11] Linkages between Central Asian terrorist movements like the Islamic Movement of Uzbekistan (IMU) and the Islamic Jihad Union (IJU) with the Taliban, and subsequently with the Al Qaida and now the ISIS, has threatened the territorial integrity and social fabric of all the Central Asian states.[12]

Central Asian terrorist groups have become increasingly active in areas in the region impacted by the Haqqani network and Tehrik-e-Taliban in Pakistan, targeting Central Asia as well as India.

---

9 'War in Progress' by Raymond Bonner, *The New York Times*, dated 10 August 2008. Available at http://www.nytimes.com/2008/08/10/books/review/Bonner-t.ht

10 'UNMOT Background', United Nations. Available at http://www.un.org/en/peacekeeping/missions/past/unmot/UnmotB.htm

11 For the nuances of this term, see 'Turkistan', Encyclopedia Britannica. Available at https://www.britannica.com/place/Turkistan

12 'Central Eurasia and Central Asia Terrorism' in Counter-Terrorism Guide published by the United States National Counter Terrorism Centre. Available at https://www.nctc.gov/site/groups/central_eurasia.html

Calibrated by sophisticated state sponsorship from Pakistan's Inter-Services Intelligence (ISI),[13] terrorism in the region has become an ongoing threat to regional security.

This has directly impacted on India and catalysed the first steps in counter-terrorism cooperation on a bilateral basis between India and Central Asia. The dissolution of the Soviet Union coincided with the first arrivals of foreign terrorist fighters in India's Jammu and Kashmir state from 1989 onwards. The abduction of western tourists in Jammu and Kashmir, and the beheading of one of them in 1994, presaged the brutal violence that has become the staple of terrorist activities today.[14] In the 1990s, India and Tajikistan worked together to support the Northern Alliance in Afghanistan against the Taliban, including through a medical facility set up by the Indian army at Farkhor, where the mortally wounded Afghan leader Ahmed Shah Massoud was taken for treatment on 9 September 2001.[15] In 2003, two key Central Asian states, Uzbekistan[16] and Tajikistan[17], set up joint working groups with India to counter terrorism.

Cooperation to counter security threats is today an integral part and priority of India's foreign policy. India's Connect Central Asia

13 'The ISI and Terrorism: Behind the Accusations', Council on Foreign Relations Backgrounder, New York, May 2011. Available at http://www.cfr.org/pakistan/isi-terrorism-behind-accusations/p11644

14 'Who took me hostage?' by Kim Housego, *The Independent*, 4 February 1997. Available at http://www.independent.co.uk/life-style/who-took-me-hostage-1276790.html

15 'A perspective on the India-Tajik Strategic Partnership', by Shri Raj Kumar Sharma, published in the Journal of the United Service Institution of India, Vol. CXLIV, No. 598, October-December 2014.

16 Ramakant, Ramakant. "Indian Prime Minister's Visit to Uzbekistan." IDSA. April 25, 2006. Accessed September 01, 2018. https://idsa.in/idsastrategiccomments/IndianPrimeMinistersVisittoUzbekistan_RDwivedi_250406.

17 Roy, Meena Singh. "India and Tajikistan: Building a Long-Term Strategic ..." IDSA. September 18, 2012. Accessed September 6, 2018. Accessed on September 01, 2018 from https://idsa.in/idsacomments/IndiaandTajikistanBuildingalongtermStrategicPartnership_MeenaSRoy_180912

policy, announced in June 2012, which was enhanced during Prime Minister Narendra Modi's historic visit to all the five countries of Central Asia in mid-2015, specifically states: "We will strengthen our strategic and security cooperation. We already have strategic partnerships in place with some Central Asian countries. In focus will be military training, joint research, counter-terrorism coordination and close consultations on Afghanistan."[18]

India's response to countering this threat also includes a pro-active use of Central Asia's Islamic heritage. As Prime Minister Modi said during his visit to Central Asia, "The Islamic heritage of both India and Central Asia is defined by the highest ideals of Islam – knowledge, piety, compassion and welfare. This is a heritage founded on the principle of love and devotion. And, it has always rejected the forces of extremism. Today, this is an important source of strength that brings India and Central Asia together."[19]

Regional response through the Shanghai Cooperation Organisation

The prospects for intensified cooperation between India and Central Asia in [20]countering the challenges posed to regional security by terrorism and religious extremism extend beyond bilateral interaction into the regional and international spheres. This was highlighted during the Sixth Ministerial Conference of the Heart of Asia process, held in Amritsar on 4 December 2016. India and the five Central Asian countries participated actively in this conference,

---

18 "India's Connect Central Asia Policy", Ministry of External Affairs, India. 12 June 2012. Available at http://www.mea.gov.in/Speeches-Statements. htm?dtl/19791/Keynote+address+by+MOS+Shri+E+Ahamed+at+First+India Central+Asia+Dialogue

19 Text of Address by PM at Nasarbayev University, Astana, Kasakhstan, on 7 July 2015. Available at http://www.narendramodi.in/text-of-address-by-pm-at-nasarbayev-university-astana-kasakhstan-183692

20 "India's Connect Central Asia Policy", Ministry of External Affairs, India. 12 June 2012. Available at http://www.mea.gov.in/Speeches- Statements. htm?dtl/19791/Keynote+address+by+MOS+Shri+E+Ahamed+at+First+India Central +Asia+Dialogue

which recognised that "terrorism is the biggest threat to peace, stability and cooperation in our region."[21]

The regional approach of Central Asia has focused on the Regional Anti-Terrorism Structure (RATS) of the Shanghai Cooperation Organisation (SCO), whose Executive Committee is based in Tashkent (Uzbekistan) as a "permanent body" of the SCO. The only other SCO "permanent body" is the SCO Secretariat based in Beijing (China).

India's interest in closer cooperation with the SCO on countering terrorist threats common to Central Asia and India were prioritised at the 2014 SCO Summit by India. In her statement, India's External Affairs Minister said, "India has long been a victim of terrorism. We are acutely aware of the threat that its perpetrators pose to our people, as also to our common region. We are seeing different theaters getting interconnected through terror networks and a globalisation of the supply chain of ideology, radicalisation, recruitment, training and financing of terrorism. This requires a resolute and more comprehensive response from the international community. We are of the firm view that only multilateral efforts and integrated actions can help effectively counter these negative forces including the related evils of drug trafficking and small arms proliferation. In this context, we are keen to deepen our security-related cooperation with the SCO in general and with the Regional Counter-Terrorism Structure, in particular."[22] India's full membership of the SCO since the SCO Summit in Qingdao (China) held in June 2018 provides a new framework for cooperation on counter-terrorism and regional security between India and Central Asia.

21 'Amritsar Declaration at the 6th Ministerial Conference of the Heart of Asia', paragraph 14. Available at http://www.mea.gov.in/bilateraldocuments. htm?dtl/27746/Amritsar+Declaration+at+the+6th+Ministerial+Conference+o f+Heart+of+Asia+December+04+2016

22 Statement by External Affairs Minister at the SCO Summit 2014 in Dushanbe, 12 September 2014. Available at https://www.mea.gov.in/Speeches-Statements.htm?dtl/23993/statement+by+external+affairs+minister+at+the+s hanghai+cooperation+organisation+sco+heads+of+state+summit+2014+in+d ushanbe

Currently headed by Russia (for the next three years), the focus of RATS is on the following six areas:

1. Maintaining working relations with competent institutions of the member states and international organisations tackling issues of fighting terrorism, separatism and extremism;

2. Assistance in interaction among the member states in preparation and staging of counter-terrorism exercises at the request of concerned member states,preparation and conduct of search operations and other activities in the field of fighting terrorism, separatism and extremism;

3. Joint drafting of international legal documents concerning the fight against terrorism, separatism and extremism;

4. Gathering and analysis of information coming to the RATS from the member states, formation and filling of RATS data bank;

5. Joint formation of a system of effective response to global challenges and threats;

6. Preparation and holding of scientific conferences and workshops, assistance in sharing experience in the field of fighting terrorism, separatism and extremism.[23]

India has held detailed consultations with RATS on counter-terrorism issues even when it was an observer in the SCO. With India's full membership of the SCO, it is possible to significantly increase this cooperation. The effectiveness of regional cooperation within this framework will depend on the demonstrated ability of all participating states to fulfill their legal obligations under international law to cooperate in countering terrorism. A priority to establish the legal framework for this would be the discussion, negotiation and adoption of a SCO convention on countering terrorism that focuses on the well-established legal principle of "prosecute or extradite",

---

23 Regional Anti-Terrorist Structure, Shanghai Cooperation Organisation. Available at http://eng.sectsco.org/structure/#6

which has been upheld by the International Court of Justice.[24]

International response through the United Nations

On the international plane, Central Asia became the first region to implement the United Nations' Global Counter Terrorism Strategy (GCTS), adopted by the UN General Assembly by consensus in September 2006.[25] India played an active role in the United Nations General Assembly discussions leading up to the adoption of the GCTS. In its remarks made when the GCTS was adopted, India reiterated its belief that "a strong response to terrorism requires broad-based international cooperation, reducing the space for terrorists, and increasing the capability of States to address terrorist threats. It requires sustained and specific cooperation by a variety of national, regional and global agencies."[26]

Based on four pillars (addressing conditions conducive to the spread of terrorism, preventing and combating terrorism, capacity building of states, and ensuring human rights and the rule of law), the GCTS enabled Central Asia to draw up a Joint Plan of Action (JPA), adopted in Ashgabat (Turkmenistan) in November 2011.[27] India participated as one of the countries at the meeting which adopted the JPA, along with Afghanistan, Azerbaijan, China, Iran, Norway, Pakistan, Russia, Turkey and the United States.

Under the JPA, four Central Asian states (with Uzbekistan deciding to have observer status) agreed to take several forward-looking counter-terrorism measures. A special focus was placed on

---

24 See "Questions relating to the Obligation to Prosecute or Extradite (Belgium vs. Senegal), International Court of Justice, 20 July 2012. Available at https://www.icj-cij.org/en/case/144

25 UN Global Counter Terrorism Strategy, 8 September 2006. Available at https://www.un.org/counterterrorism/ctitf/en/un-global-counter-terrorism-strategy

26 *Statement by India at the UN General Assembly* at the adoption of the GCTS, 8 September 2006. Available at https://www.pminewyork.org/pdf/uploadpdf/49861ind1245.pdf

27 The Joint Plan of Action for Central Asia, 30 November 2011. Available at https://unrcca.unmissions.org/joint-plan-action

stabilizing the situation in Afghanistan, seen by Central Asian states as the primary source for the terrorist threats to their security. The JPA gives details of Central Asian policy in this context, including the coordination of initiatives such as the delivery of electricity, construction of railways, cooperation on counter-terrorism and counter-narcotics, strengthening the agriculture system for alternative livelihoods, sharing information on terrorist organisations and criminal groups, cross-border cooperation, provision of mutual legal assistance in criminal matters, exchange of best practices, as well as joint training and exercises.

Addressing the situation within Central Asia, the JPA prioritised national development strategies on youth, women, returning migrants and other vulnerable groups of population in initiatives for education, sustainable human development, social justice, including fighting poverty, and social inclusion to reduce their marginalisation and vulnerability to violent extremism and recruitment by terrorists.

It supported the institutionalisation of inter-ethnic dialogue, and the promotion of inter-faith dialogue to prevent disinformation that could lead to radicalisation. Central Asian states resolved to provide support for religious institutions, as needed, operating within the framework of existing legislation, through specialised training courses and exchanges with other countries beyond the region.

The United Nations Counter-Terrorism Implementation Task Force or CTITF is responsible for implementing the JPA. It has held three meetings so far on Central Asia, focusing on dialogue with religious institutions and leaders in preventing conflicts and countering extremism (Almaty, November 2013), engaging the media in countering terrorism (Bishkek, July 2014) and border security and management for countering terrorism (Asghabat, March 2015). These developments enabled the UN General Assembly to adopt a resolution on "Strengthening regional and international cooperation to ensure peace, stability and sustainable development in the Central Asian region" on 22 June 2018, which was introduced by Uzbekistan.[28]

---

28 UN General Assembly Resolution A/RES/72/283 dated 22 June 2018.

The United Nations General Assembly resolution specifically noted the important role that regional cooperation on countering terrorism plays in the overall framework of peace, security and development of Central Asia, pointing to the positive impact of the first Central Asian Heads of State Summit held in Astana in March 2018, the Samarkand Conference committing Central Asian states to intensify regional cooperation in November 2017, and the Dushanbe Conference on countering terrorism and violent extremism held in May 2018. India has supported the adoption of this resolution, which prioritises the effort of preventive diplomacy in responding to security challenges to Central Asia.

Transnational Crime and Drug Trafficking

The two other major threats to the security of Central Asia identified by the states of the region are transnational crime and drug trafficking. These threats have been discussed bilaterally between India and the Central Asian states on a regular basis. As a result of these discussions, bilateral cooperation in preventing the financing of criminal activities, including terrorism, and interdicting of illegal drugs has become part of India's broader security cooperation with Central Asia.

As with countering terrorism and religious extremism, this bilateral cooperation has been enhanced by India's participation in the regional and international structures created to address such challenges.

As far as drug trafficking is concerned, the United Nations assesses that "Afghanistan continues to dominate the worldwide opium market. In 2015, the country still accounted for almost two thirds of the global area under illicit opium poppy cultivation. Most of Europe is supplied with Afghan opiates, with the "northern route", from Afghanistan to neighbouring States in Central Asia, the Russian Federation and other countries of the Commonwealth of Independent States, starting to undergo a resurgence after a decline

---

Available at https://undocs.org/en/A/RES/72/283

in the period 2008-2012".[29] Cooperation between India and Central Asia on countering the threat posed by drug trafficking has focused on exchanging information on this aspect, as well as on cooperating together to assist Afghanistan to overcome this challenge.

Regionally, apart from the potential cooperation within the SCO following India's full membership from 2017, India cooperates with Central Asia in the framework of the regional Eurasia Group (EAG). This grouping comprises of Belarus, China, India, Kazakhstan, Kyrgyzstan, Russian Federation, Tajikistan, Turkmenistan and Uzbekistan. The EAG plays an important role in combating the threat of terrorism and increasing the transparency and security of financial systems of the region. The EAG objective is to incorporate these countries into the global system on anti-money laundering and combating the financing of terrorism (AML/CFT). The EAG is a regional body that became an Associate Member of the Financial Action Task Force or FATF in June 2010.[30]

Within the United Nations framework, India collaborates actively with Central Asia through the United Nations Office on Drugs and Crime or UNODC. A Central Asian presence of the UNODC began in Tashkent in 1993, which provided the nucleus for opening separate UNODC offices in all five Central Asian states. UNODC's activities have a "traditional emphasis on building capacity in counter-narcotics through technical assistance", linking "national projects on border control with regional projects developing intelligence analysis systems and joint operations. These include: the Central Asia Regional Information and Coordination Centre in Almaty, precursor chemical control, border liaison office project, national drug control agencies and intelligence lead policing."[31]

---

29 United Nations Office on Drugs and Crime (UNODC). Available at https://www.unodc.org/unodc/en/drug-trafficking/central-asia.html

30 For further details on the EAG's activities, see https://eurasiangroup.org/en

31 For further details see UNODC Central Asia website, available at https://www.unodc.org/centralasia/en/unodc-in-central-asia.html

Conclusion

As will be evident from this assessment, India's overall perception of the challenges and prospects of regional security in Central Asia is to identify the common sources of such challenges, and work together with the Central Asian states bilaterally, regionally and internationally, to counter them. The mutual benefit of such cooperation has been embedded into India's national security interests, which looks at the region of Central Asia as an integral part of India's extended neighbourhood. With new connectivity links bringing the populations of Central Asia and India closer, this link of shared interests and a shared destiny will propel greater collaboration between India and Central Asia, contributing constructively to creating an "Asian Century".

SECTION – II

Role and Approach of Uzbekistan in Conflict Resolution and Peace Building in Afghanistan – Uzbekistan's view

Bakhtiyor Mustafayev

When we state that Central Asia is the main priority of Uzbekistan's foreign policy, we also consider development of relations with neighboring Afghanistan. Today, nobody can deny that the conflict in Afghanistan remains one of the topical issues of ensuring regional and international security.

Analysis shows that the military-political situation in Afghanistan remains turbulent and controversial, evidenced by strengthening of confrontation between Kabul and the Taliban movement, expanding presence of the "Islamic State" on the Afghan soil, the deterioration of the socio-economic situation, increase in drug production.

The current difficult situation in Afghanistan, therefore, requires a thoughtful assessment of the internal situation and the following merit consideration for its solution.

Firstly, the result of efforts of the international community, undertaken for more than three decades have convincingly demonstrated that there is no military solution to Afghan Conflict. The only way for establishing peace is a direct dialogue between the opposing sides.

At the same time, one important thing is that the Afghans themselves should suggest a format of future negotiations, and negotiations should take place without putting forward any preconditions by the sides under the auspices of the United Nations.

Secondly, today the Afghan conflict has become fully international; its content and structure have changed fundamentally.

In this regard, in addition to forming an intra-Afghan consensus, it is necessary to form a consensus at the regional level, and develop an understanding for a common approach among the extra-regional players. With the new hotspots emerging in other regions of the world, it is imperative the Afghan issue should not be relegated to a lower priority in the international agenda.

Thirdly, the most important condition for stabilising the situation in Afghanistan, along with a political settlement, is the integration of the country into global economy, including regional economy of Central Asia. We should consider Afghanistan not as a problem, but as an opportunity, as a new prospect for mutually beneficial regional cooperation[1]. All these meet fundamental interests of the Central and South Asia countries, opening a strategic opportunity for realising all existing potential in spheres such as trade, economic and cultural-humanitarian cooperation, to make a "breakthrough" in the field of transport communications.

The development of the trans-Afghan corridor will have a positive impact for the access of Central Asian countries, to the ports of South Asia, the Persian Gulf and the Middle East. In this context, Uzbekistan, considering intensification of the political dialogue, trade-economic and cultural-humanitarian cooperation as the most effective factor in the settlement of the situation in Afghanistan, has taken concrete practical measures to intensify bilateral cooperation.

During the several meetings with leaders of foreign countries, including the President of Afghanistan, as well as in his speeches, the President of the Republic of Uzbekistan Shavkat Mirziyoyev outlined that Uzbekistan remains committed to conducting a friendly and pragmatic policy towards Afghanistan.

Thanks to the serious intentions of the parties to build constructive and friendly relations, over the past year the cooperation

---

1   Afghan conflict can be settled only on basis of intra-Afghan national accord. https://www.uzdaily.com/articles-id-37004.htm

of Uzbekistan and Afghanistan has received a new impetus, which is unprecedented.

High level contacts - meetings of the heads of states, ministries and departments have become regular. President of Uzbekistan Shavkat Mirziyoyev and Afghan leader Ashraf Ghani met in the framework of the SCO and the Organisation of Islamic Cooperation (OIC) Astana summits, and the UN General Assembly (New York).

In this context, it should be noted that the establishment of the institution of the Special Representative of the President of the Republic of Uzbekistan in Afghanistan in May 2017 underlines the special approach of the Uzbek leadership to the development of comprehensive relations with Afghanistan.

During the visit of the Afghan President A. Ghani to Uzbekistan in December 2017, the two sides agreed on the launch of the project for the construction of the Surkhan-Puli Khumri railway line and the Mazar-e-Sharif-Herat railway. 20 documents and 40 export contracts worth more than 500 million dollars were also signed. During the meeting, Uzbekistan granted to Afghanistan 25 Isuzu buses and 3 New Holland modern tractors as a sign of sincere friendship between the two countries.

Compared to 2002, the volume of electricity supplies from Uzbekistan to Afghanistan has increased 30 times. Since January 2018, Uzbekistan has lowered the price of electricity supplied to Afghanistan from 7 to 5 cents. This and the Surkhan-Puli Khumri transmission line will help solve energy shortages and create new enterprises and jobs in Afghanistan.

Moreover, the construction of the new Mazar-e-Sharif-Herat railway will also make a significant contribution to the economic reconstruction of Afghanistan.

According to preliminary data, after the launch of the railway, the trade turnover of the Afghanistan should increase by 50 per cent, and the projected volume of cargo transit would be about 5 million tons per year. Since 2017, the volume of trade has increased by 15 per cent, amounting to about 600 million USD[2]. This initiative by the President of Uzbekistan on the development of Uzbek-Afghan cooperation would significantly increase the trade turnover and bring its volume to 1.5 billion USD in the coming years.

In order to enhance the cooperation between the two states, an international logistics centre with a customs terminal was established in Termez. This dry port aimed to facilitate export-import and transit traffic between two countries, and with access to the markets of Europe and Asia.

Considering the key role of the education of Afghan citizens in ensuring security and stability in Afghanistan, an educational centre was opened in Termez (Surkhandarya region) in January this year, where Afghan young people would be trained in two, four and six-year full-time study programs in 17 courses of higher and 16 courses of secondary specialised education. During the opening of the Centre, the first batch of 110 Afghan students was enrolled for the courses in Uzbek language and literature[3]. It is planned to increase the intake to 300 students in future.

A fresh impetus was given to the interaction between the law enforcement agencies of Uzbekistan and Afghanistan to discuss topical issues of regional security. Towards the end, the first meeting of the Uzbek-Afghan joint commission on security issues was held in February 2018 in Tashkent.

Uzbekistan has also taken specific political and diplomatic measures aimed at peaceful settlement of the Afghan crisis. Under this initiative a high-level international conference on Afghanistan "Peace process, cooperation in the sphere of security and regional interaction" was held in Tashkent on 27 March 2018.

The event was closely followed by many decision makers of

---

2   High dynamics of Uzbek-Afghan relations is the result of the new foreign policy strategy of the President of the Republic of Uzbekistan. http://ut.uz/en/politics/eldor-aripov-high-dynamics-of-uzbek-afghan-relations-is-the-result-of-the-new-foreign-policy-strateg/

3   Educational Centre on training Afghan citizens opens in Uzbekistan. https://www.uzdaily.com/articles-id-42457.htm

foreign countries. The proposal to hold the international conference in Uzbekistan and the need to combine efforts aimed at ensuring peace and stability in the Afghanistan are conditioned by the following factors[4]:

First, the initiative to hold the conference was an integral part of Uzbekistan's overall strategy to ensure regional security and stability.

Second, for thousands of years, the people of Uzbekistan and Afghanistan have lived in the same cultural and civilisational space. Historically Uzbekistan and Afghanistan have close political, trade, economic and cultural ties;[5]

Third, Uzbekistan is strongly committed to the principle of interdependence and indivisibility of security. From this point of view, the security of Afghanistan and that of Uzbekistan is interlinked, as also the stability and prosperity of the entire region of Central and South Asia.

Fourth, Uzbekistan has had experience in promoting the peace process in Afghanistan. In 1999, by the initiative of the Uzbek side, the "6+2" Group met in Tashkent at the ministerial level (neighboring countries of Afghanistan, Russia and the United States). The representatives of the Northern Alliance and the Taliban movement had also participated in this meeting. Following the talks, the Tashkent Declaration was adopted on the basic principles for the Peaceful Settlement of the Conflict in Afghanistan, which became the only official document, agreed and accepted by all the domestic political forces Afghanistan, and was also approved by the UN.

In March 2018, the Tashkent Conference on Afghanistan adopted the final declaration, which included the following[6]:

---

4 Address by the President of the Republic of Uzbekistan Shavkat Mirziyoyev at the international conference on Afghanistan «Peace process, security cooperation and regional connectivity». http://usa.uz/en/politics/address-by-the-president-of-the-republic-of-uzbekistan-shavk-27-03-2018

5 Ш.Абдуллаев. Исторические и культурно-цивилизационные взаимосвязи народов Узбекистана и Афганистана.

6 Declaration of the Tashkent Conference on Afghanistan: Peace Process,

1) support the proposals of Afghan government on launching direct negotiations with Taliban without any preconditions;

2) guaranteeing the inclusion of the Taliban in the political process as a legitimate political actor;

3) adopting a "road map" by international community in order to assist the process of national reconciliation and socio-economic development in Afghanistan;

4) recognition of the importance of international and regional initiatives to ensure peace and stability in Afghanistan.

In this context, the active participation of the Indian delegation headed by the Minister of State for Foreign Affairs Mobashar Javed Akbar at the international conference on Afghanistan at Tashkent is considered by the Uzbekistan as an important factor in consolidating the efforts of the international community in establishing peace and stability in Afghanistan.

Uzbekistan welcomes India's efforts in addressing the crisis in Afghanistan, particularly in the areas of education and training of military personnel, and the restoration and implementation of infrastructure projects. Tashkent supports the revitalisation of India's policy in Afghanistan and advocates for increasing its effectiveness. Today Uzbekistan has all necessary capabilities to implement joint projects with India on virtually all issues aimed at ensuring stability and sustainable development of Afghanistan.

There are three areas of joint India-Uzbek projects in Afghanistan. First is India's participation in the construction of the Mazar-e-Sharif-Herat railway. This project can be seen as a continuation of the previously constructed "Hairatan-Mazar-e-Sharif" by Uzbekistan, the first railway line that is of key importance for the Afghan economy. The creation of the transport corridor Mazar-e-Sharif-Herat with access to the Iranian ports Chabahar and Bandar Abbas will allow India to get the shortest access to the markets of Afghanistan, Central Asia and the CIS.

Security Cooperation and Regional Connectivity. http://usa.uz/en/politics/declaration-of-the-tashkent-conference-on-afghanistan-peace--28-03-2018

Due to the lack of direct connectivity, trade between India and the Central Asian states is far below its potential, and does not exceed 1.1 per cent. India has invested 500 million US dollars for the development of the port infrastructure at Chabahar, and is participating in the construction of the Iranian-Afghan railway line as part of the development of the Chabahar-Zahedan-Saranj Southern Trade Corridor, as also the Afghanistan main road connecting the large Afghan cities as Herat, Kandahar, Kabul and Mazar-e-Sharif.

Secondly, there could be cooperation between Uzbekistan and India in the training of Afghan civil and military personnel. In this context, it is noteworthy that India is one of the key states in the training of military personnel in Afghanistan. In recent years, more than 4,000 Afghan officers have been trained in Indian military institutions. This year the figure is expected to increase their number by 50 per cent[7].

Education stimulates the aspirations for self-improvement among youths in the Afghan society, and a key factor for achieving sustainable and stable development. In this regard, it is relevant to support India and jointly promote the initiative of the President of the Republic of Uzbekistan to establish a special International Fund for the Support of Education in Afghanistan.

Third is the Uzbekistan and India joint effort in the provision of medical services to the Afghan population. According to the United Nations Health Organisation, about 100-110 thousand people die each year from various diseases for lack of necessary health services and medicines in Afghanistan. In this context, currently 7 free economic zones (FEZ) specialising in the production of pharmaceutical products operate in Uzbekistan and one of them – "Boysun Farm" is located on the border with Afghanistan Surkhandarya region. In this regard, taking into account the logistics and favorable conditions created in Uzbekistan for foreign investors, creation of joint Uzbek-

---

7   "Strengthening India-Afghanistan Strategic Relations in an Uncertain World" Address by H.E. Shaida Abdali, Ambassador of Afghanistan to India. https://www.brookings.edu/events/india-afghanistan-and-connectivity-in-south-asia-address-by-h-e-shaida-abdali-ambassador-of-afghanistan-to-india/ Apr 25, 2017

Indian enterprises for production of medicines based on the needs of the Afghans can make a significant contribution to improving the health situation in Afghanistan.

In general, it should be noted that Uzbekistan would continue its practical assistance in creating the infrastructure of Afghanistan, considering this as an indispensable condition for promoting peace and prosperity in the country. The fact that ensuring security in Afghanistan is a decisive factor not only in regional but also global security context, Uzbekistan is ready to recognise and support any political processes that are aimed at maintaining peace and stability in Afghanistan.

Role and Appraoch of India in Conflict Resolution and Peace Building in Afghanistan: India's View

Major General BK Sharma, AVSM, SM and Bar (Retd)

Introduction

From the dawn of history Afghanistan has remained at the centre–stage of peace and conflict in the Indian subcontinent. The 'Old Silk' Route formed the crucible of trade, science, spirituality and cross-fertilisation of civilisations, connecting the Indian sub-continent-Central Asia-West Asia and China. On the flip side, many invasions; led notably by Alexander, Tamerlane, Ghauri, Ghaznvi, and Babur, staged through Afghanistan into India thus redrawing the sociopolitical landscape of the region. Afghanistan was the fulcrum of the first 'Great Game' of the 19th century between the British India and the Russian Empire. The two great powers realised the futility of subjugating Afghanistan and settled for creating it as a buffer state The second 'Great Game' in the Eighties between the US - Saudi Arabia - Pakistan alliance against the Soviet Union legitimsed the use of Islamist Jihad as an instrument of state policy. Post the US exit, the Af-Pak region emerged as the epicentre of International terrorism. In the fall of eighties, Pakistan's military establishment directed Afghan trained Jihadists to wage a proxy war in Kashmir. The third 'Great Game' began in the wake of 9/11 that saw the ouster of Taliban regime and onset of democracy in Afghanistan, albeit in the midst of a virulent conflict unleashed by Pakistan sponsored Taliban and hosts of other militant groups, including Islamic State of Khorasan Province (ISKP). Talibanistan of Afghanistan or spread of rabid Wahabi – Salafi ideology does not bode well for regional peace and stability.

Afghanistan is at the cross–roads of its strategic destiny. Geo-strategically, Afghanistan is a landlocked country with access to the outside world through the North Distribution Network to the North through Central Asia or Bolan and Khyber Passes to the South in Pakistan or Chabahar– Saranj- Delaram Axis or International North South Transit Corridor (INSTC) to the west in Iran. At the same time, it enjoys a distinction of being a strategic bridge for inter-regional connectivity and pan-regional energy corridors that if successful can potentially alter the politico-economic landscape of the region, transforming it into a zone of co – prosperity. But if Afghanistan fails, it will become a major source of regional instability and dampen the prospects of smooth operationalisation of Belt and Road corridors, China Pakistan Economic Corridor (CPEC), Lapis Lazuli transport corridor, Persian Gulf Corridor (Ashgabat Agreement), Afghanistan-Pakistan-Tajikistan Trade and Transit Agreement and Pan-Energy grids such as The Turkmenistan–Afghanistan–Pakistan–India Pipeline (TAPI) pipeline and CASA -1000 power grid. The aforesaid trade and energy corridors are vital for India's access to Eurasia and to diversify sources of energy imports. India aspires to see the transformation of conflict–ridden Afghanistan into a stable and democratic state under an Afghan owned and Afghan led peace process' that is duly supported by the regional countries and the international community. It would, therefore, be in order to examine the evolving scenario in Afghanistan, analyse its impact on India's strategic interests and dilate on India's strategic engagement with Afghanistan.

Politico – Economic Scenario

Fragile State. Decades of instability and violence have turned Afghanistan into a very fragile state; ranking 9th lowest in fragile state index, and 169th in Human Development Index out of 188 countries[1]. As per Transparency International, in terms of corruption index, Afghanistan stands at 177 out of 180 countries[2]. Afghanistan

---

1 "Afghanistan Human Development Indicators." Human Development Reports. Accessed August 29, 2018. http://hdr.undp.org/en/countries/profiles/AFG.

2 "Afghanistan Report - Corruption Perception Index" Transparency International. Transparency International - The Global Anti-Corruption

performed poor in the ease of doing business index, ranking 183 out of 190 countries[3]. According to Turkmenistan–Afghanistan–Pakistan–India Pipeline (TAPI) 63.7, percent of the population is below 25 years and is facing very high unemployment levels[4]. According to the 2018 Women, Peace and Security Index, Afghanistan along with Syria are the worst places to be a woman[5]. Women in Afghanistan still face serious justice and security constraints. According to the Ministry of Labor, Social Affairs, Martyrs and Disabled, two million Afghans are unemployed in the country[6]. Poverty is further compounding the problem, the UN Office for Coordination of Humanitarian Affairs (OCHA) estimates at least two million Afghans are at risk of starvation due to drought[7]. The economy is in regression since 2012, and foreign aid contributes to 90 of the country's GDP[8]. The violence has taken a very heavy toll of precious human lives. A total of 10,453 civilian casualties - 3,438

Coalition. Accessed August 29, 2018. https://www.transparency.org/country/AFG.

3 "Doing Business in Afghanistan - World Bank Group." Doing Business in Switserland - World Bank Group. Accessed August 29, 2018. http://www.doingbusiness.org/data/exploreeconomies/afghanistan.

4 "UNFPA Afghanistan | Young People." UNFPA Afghanistan | Child Marriage. March 08, 2018. Accessed August 30, 2018. https://afghanistan.unfpa.org/en/node/15227.

5 Rajagopalan, Swarna, and WRN Core. "Women, Peace and Security Index." WOMENS REGIONAL NETWORK. May 11, 2018. Accessed August 29, 2018. https://www.womensregionalnetwork.org/single-post/2018/03/07/Women-Peace-and-Security-Index.

6 Omid, Haidarshah. "ADB Concerned Over Growing Poverty In Afghanistan RAWA News." Filmed by RAWA: Taliban Publicly Execute an Afghan Woman. April 12, 2018. Accessed August 30, 2018. http://www.rawa.org/temp/runews/2018/04/12/adb-concerned-over-growing-poverty-in-afghanistan.html

7 "2 Million at Risk of Food Insecurity in Afghanistan, Warns UN." Qatar-Tribune. May 27, 2018. Accessed August 30, 2018. http://www.qatar-tribune.com/news-details/id/126542

8 "Economics and Business/industry." The Swedish Committee for Afghanistan (SCA). May 22, 2018. Accessed August 30, 2018. https://swedishcommittee.org/afghanistan/economy

people were killed and 7,015 injured in 2017. More than 32,000 civilians lost their lives or suffered injuries since 2015[9]. The sectarian violence against the Shia communities has been steadily increasing in Afghanistan. The refugee crisis is worsening as Afghans comprise the largest protracted refugee population in Asia, and the second largest refugee population in the world[10].

Political Instability. Afghanistan's parliamentary and district council elections are scheduled on 20 October 2018, followed by the presidential elections in 2019. The government and the Independent Election Commission (IEC) are facing twin challenges, apart from the problems like fraud, rigging etc. First, there are public protests against the election commission for banning dosens of Afghan strongmen and lawmakers from running for parliament[11]. Second, rising level of attacks on voter registration centres. There are simmering differences between the President and Chief Executive and in the cabinet as seen from spate resignations of ministers holding high portfolios[12]. Warlord factionalism is adding to political chaos. Former Governor of Balkh Province Atta Mohammad Noor has formed a Grand National Coalition of Afghanistan, which includes Jamiat-e-Islami, the National Unity of People of Afghanistan and National Islamic Movement of Afghanistan, led by

---

9 "Afghanistan: 10,000 Civilian Casualties in 2017 - UN Report Suicide Attacks and IEDS Caused High Number of Deaths and Injuries." UNAMA. February 15, 2018. Accessed August 30, 2018. https://unama.unmissions.org/afghanistan-10000-civilian-casualties-2017-un-report-suicide-attacks-and-ieds-caused-high-number

10 United Nations. "Afghanistan." UNHCR. Accessed August 30, 2018. http://www.unhcr.org/afghanistan.html

11 Jain, Rupam. "Afghan Bid to Weed out Suspect Candidates Spells More Election Trouble." Reuters. August 22, 2018. Accessed August 30, 2018. https://in.reuters.com/article/afghanistan-election/afghan-bid-to-weed-out-suspect-candidates-spells-more-election-trouble-idINKCN1L70U1

12 "Afghanistan Political Turmoil Deepens as Regional Leader Ousted." Reuters. December 20, 2017. Accessed August 29, 2018. https://www.reuters.com/article/us-afghanistan-politics/afghanistan-political-turmoil-deepens-as-regional-leader-ousted-idUSKBN1EE16A

first Vice President Abdul Rashid Dostum[13].Another new political group Called 'Mehwar-e Mardom-e Afghanistan' is known to have links with former President Karzai,[14] who has taken strident anti US stance. How these political alignments pan out will have an impact on the political stability in the country.

Security Scenario

Ecology of Terror. Afghanistan ranks very high in the terrorism index (2 out of 163)[15].Out of 98 globally recognised terrorist groups, about 20 such groups are operating in the Af-Pak region. They are adherents of extremist Wahabi-Salafi ideology. They want to create a Caliphate based on Sharia or Nisam e Mustafa. The cliché that, "Americans have the watches, whereas, we have the time" demonstrates their resolve for a protracted conflict to fulfill their goals. There are a multitude of extremist groups (local, regional and global Jihadists), based in Afghanistan and on the Pakistan side of Durand line. The Taliban has launched operation KHANDAQ to target major communication centres, government installations, foreign nationals and voter registration centres[16]. Special Inspector General for Afghanistan Reconstruction (SIGAR) report claims that 13.8 per cent of Afghanistan's districts are under insurgent control, an increase of 1 per cent from same period in 2017. Government controls 58.5 per cent of Afghanistan's total land area, down by

---

13 Salangi, Abdul Wadood. "Launch Of New Coalition Meets With Mixed Reaction." TOLOnews. July 27, 2018. Accessed August 30, 2018. https://www.tolonews.com/afghanistan/launch-new-coalition-meets-mixed-reaction.

14 "Afghanistan: Background and U.S. Policy" In US Congressional Research Service. May 1, 2018. Accessed August 30 2018.https://www.everycrsreport.com/files/20180501_R45122_aa2ec56eb7b9eea1d00276f5c3d05d3bd4c5bd5c.pdf

15 "Global Terrorism Index (GTI)." Study of Terrorism and Responses to Terrorism (START). Accessed August 28, 2018. https://reliefweb.int/sites/reliefweb.int/files/resources/Globalper cent20Terrorismper cent20Indexper cent202017per cent20per cent284per cent29.pdf

16 "Taliban Launch Spring Offensive Codenamed Al Khandaq." Pajhwok. April 25, 2018. Accessed August 30, 2018. https://www.pajhwok.com/en/2018/04/25/taliban-launch-spring-offensive-codenamed-al-khandaq

1 per cent from previous quarter[17]. The militants have intensified their activities in relatively peaceful north and western parts of Afghanistan including recent attacks on the city of Gazni[18]. This is evident from two attempts by the Jihadists to seise Kunduz in 2015-2016 and reports of a series of attacks in northern towns Jowzjan, Faryab and Badghis[19]. The Taliban are mostly active in the rural areas and control about 12 percent of population. ISKP is active in about 30 districts and mostly indulges in sectarian killings.

Cross-border Terrorism. Pakistan's complicity in cross border terrorism remains unabated. According to noted Pakistani journalist Najam Sethi, "Pakistan's relations with Afghanistan will not improve until the Afghan Taliban are disrupted and defeated or compelled to sue for peace."[20] President Ashraf Ghani has stated on several occasions that, "Peace Initiative taken by Afghanistan with Pakistan is not successful as Pakistan differentiates between good and bad terrorists in practice".[21] Pakistan based terrorist groups like Lashkar-e-Taiba (LeT), Jaish-e-Mohammed (JeM) and Haqqani network were categorically named for regional instability at the 'Heart of Asia' conference held at Amritsar in December 2016 and in the Brazil, Russia, India, China, South Africa (BRICS) declaration made during the summit at Xiamen (China) on 04 Sep

---

17 Ariana News. "Afghan Gov't Fails to Extend Control Over Districts: SIGAR."Ariana News. August 04, 2018. Accessed August 30, 2018. https://ariananews.af/afghan-govt-fails-to-extend-control-over-districts-sigar/

18 Nordland, Rod, and Fahim Abed. "Taliban Launch Assault on Ghazni, a Key Afghan City." The New York Times. August 10, 2018. Accessed September 05, 2018. https://www.nytimes.com/2018/08/10/world/asia/afghanistan-taliban-ghazni.html.

19 Habib, Qadir, Ron Synovitz, Frud Bezhan, and Michael Scollon. "Afghanistan's New Northern Flash Points." RadioFreeEurope/RadioLiberty. Accessed August 30, 2018. https://www.rferl.org/a/27013992.html

20 Najam Sethi (2016), "Quetta Terror: Time for Pakistan to Change Its National Security Paradigm", August 13, https://thewire.in/58879/quetta-terror-time-for-pakistan-to-change-its-national-security-paradigm/

21 Peace initiatives with Pakistan remain unsuccessful, says Afghan president, July 10, 2016, http://www.dawn.com/news/1269728

2017[22][23]. President Trump while enunciating South Asia strategy on 21 Aug, 2017 bluntly stated, "We can no longer be silent about Pakistan's safe havens for terrorist organisations. We have been paying Pakistan billions and billions of dollars and at the same time they are housing the very terrorist we are fighting. That will have to change immediately[24]." In the meanwhile, Pakistan and Afghanistan have renewed Afghanistan-Pakistan Action Plan for Peace and Solidarity (APAPPS) that seeks non use and non violation of each others territory, avoid blame games and institutionalise system of joint working groups, joint check posts and exchange of liaison officers at the headquarters for coordination of efforts. Nonetheless, these initiatives have yet to render any tangible results on ground.

Reconciliation with Taliban. The Taliban has spurned President Ashraf Ghani's ceasefire offer under the Kabul Peace Process. He had extended ceasefire on the eve of Eid al-Adha effective from 20 August 2018. Earlier, he had announced a ceasefire with the Taliban during the Eid al-Fitr holiday in June, which was partially reciprocated by the Taliban[25]. The Taliban are vehement about establishing an Islamic Caliphate in Afghanistan. They do not recognise the Afghan constitution or the elected government and harp on the withdrawal of foreign troops as a precondition for

22 Subramanian, Nirupama. "Heart of Asia Conference Names Pakistan Terror Groups, Urges States to Act." The Indian Express. December 04, 2016. Accessed August 30, 2018. https://indianexpress.com/article/india/heart-of-asia-regional-meet-names-pak-terror-groups-urges-states-to-act/

23 "BRICS Leaders Xiamen Declaration: Full Text - Times of India." The Times of India. September 04, 2017. Accessed August 30, 2018. https://timesofindia.indiatimes.com/india/brics-leaders-xiamen-declaration-full-text/articleshow/60359120.cms

24 "Remarks by President Trump on the Strategy in Afghanistan and South Asia." The White House. Accessed September 05, 2018. https://www.whitehouse.gov/briefings-statements/remarks-president-trump-strategy-afghanistan-south-asia/.

25 Al Jaseera. "Afghanistan's Ghani Declares Eid Ceasefire with Taliban." Israeli–Palestinian Conflict | Al Jaseera. August 19, 2018. Accessed August 30, 2018. https://www.aljaseera.com/news/2018/08/afghanistan-ghani-declares-eid-ceasefire-taliban-180819143135061.html

talks[26]. The Taliban did not participate in the renewed Quadrilateral Coordination Group (QCG), comprising US, China, Pakistan and Afghanistan, held in Muscat on 16 Oct 2017[27]. Likewise, the Russia led (Moscow format) reconciliation initiative with Taliban remains inconclusive, so are the efforts by China to bring Taliban to the negotiation table[28]. The Taliban have remained indifferent to appeals made at the Jakarta Trilateral Religious Scholars Conference, or the Fatwa issued by Afghan clerics or urging at Mecca religious conference to shun violence and join the negotiation process. Taliban intransigence however persists.

Counter Terrorism Campaign. The Afghan National Security Force (ANSF) despite serious constraints has resisted Taliban onslaughts In Southeastern and northern provinces of Afghanistan. According to Department of Defence (DOD) Report, the ANDSF's total authorised strength was 352,000 personnel, including 227,374 ANA and 124,626 ANP personnel[29] Presently, ANSF are structured on the basis of six ANA Corps, one Kabul division, two Mobile Strike Force Brigades (MSB), one Special Operations Corps (SOC), and several Afghan National Police zones. There are about 30 commando companies deployed and 20 more companies of Special Forces are being raised. Anti-terrorist operations are being supported by Afghan Air force with a range of aircraft and helicopters such as, AF-A29-A Light AC, MI 17/35, MD 530, UH-60, Black Hawks and UAVS backed up by US/North Atlantic Treaty Organisation

---

26 Osman, Borhan, and Anand Gopal. "Taliban Views on a Future State." NYU Centre on International Cooperation. July 2016. Accessed August 30, 2018. https://cic.nyu.edu/sites/default/files/taliban_future_state_final.pdf

27 Gul, Ayaz. "Taliban Dismissive of Four-Nation Afghan Peace Talks in Oman." VOA. October 10, 2017. Accessed August 30, 2018. https://www.voanews.com/a/taliban-dismissive-of-afghan-peace-talks-in-oman/4064172.html

28 "Afghanistan Won't Attend Peace Talks in Moscow with Taliban: Government Sources." Firstpost. August 22, 2018. Accessed August 30, 2018. https://www.firstpost.com/world/afghanistan-wont-attend-peace-talks-in-moscow-with-taliban-government-sources-5023961.html

29 "SIGAR Quarterly Report- 2018." SIGAR. July 30, 2018. Accessed August 19, 2018. https://www.sigar.mil/pdf/quarterlyreports/2018-07-30qr-section3-security.pdf

(NATO) Air Superiority Fighters. Afghan National Territorial Units are being raised to replace weak local auxiliary units. The ANSF are being supported by 15653 troops (8475 from the US) and remainder from about 38 NATO/allies, deployed in Operation Sentinel (hardcore counter terrorism operations) and Operation Resolute Support Mission (Train, Advise and Assist Missions) respectively[30]. The underlining aim of Operation KHALID 2017 and Operation NUSRAT 2018 has been to prevent capture of communication centres, secure roads and developmental projects. ANSF has been fairly successful in defeating Taliban offensives in Kunduz and Gazhni provinces; however, their success against Fidayeen attacks has been lacklustre. On the whole, put in words of Gen Nicholson, a state of strategic stalemate prevails in Afghanistan.

Zero Sum Geopolitics in Afghanistan

The international community has espoused support to 'Afghan led, Afghan owned Peace Process; be it at the Warsaw Summit, Brussels International Donors Conference or declarations made at the 'Heart of Asia', BRICS and SCO summits. However, in practice, major players are adopting contradictory approaches to deal with the problem. President Trump in his South Asia policy asserts for renewed effort in combating terrorism, building ANSDF, particularly the Afghan Special Forces and Air-Force, putting pressure on Pakistan to dismantle terrorist infrastructure and solicit Indian support in peace building and development in Afghanistan. The US alleges that Russia, China, Pakistan and Iran are scuttling the US endeavors by hobnobbing with the Taliban. Moscow has for years opposed the Taliban, calling them terrorists, and supported the anti-Taliban 'Northern Alliance'. Samir Kubalov, Putin's' special representative for Afghanistan termed ISIS in Afghanistan a bigger threat than the Taliban.[31] In December 2015, a senior Russian

---

30 DoD Report, Enhancing Security and Stability in Afghanistan, Jun 2018. Accessed on August 29, 2018 from https://media.defense.gov/2018/Jul/03/2001938620/-1/-1/1/1225-REPORT-JUNE-2018-FINAL-UNCLASS-BASE.PDF

31 Pakistan Critical to Defeating ISIS, Says Russian Special Rep to Afghanistan,

diplomat declared "the Taliban interest objectively coincides with ours[32]". China perceives security in the region from the perspective of mitigating East Turkestan Islamic Movement (ETIM) threat to Xinjiang, Belt and Road corridors, energy corridors, securing investments in mining and oil exploration projects in Aynek and North Amu Darya. China is known to play the role of an interlocutor between Afghanistan and Pakistan and hobnobbing with Taliban. Iran had supported Northern alliance and the US against Taliban but is now in favour of engaging Taliban.

Strategic Implications for Regional Stability

Implications for India. Afghanistan assumes the status of a buffer and bridge in India's strategic calculus. Talibanistion or rising spectre of Islamic State in Afghanistan is a major trans-national threat that has ramifications for regional peace and stability.

India favors Afghanistan to be a rallying point for the fight against Violent Extremism. Indian Defence Minister Smt Nirmala Sitharaman addressing the 'VII Moscow Conference on International Security' from 03 to 05 April 2018 in Moscow said that persistence of instability in Afghanistan are threatening the gains made over the past few decades of growth and development in Asia. She urged the international community to adopt a policy of zero tolerance towards terrorism. She also urged to consolidate capacities of the Afghan government and security forces in the face of newer provocations and terrorism.[33] India is gravely concernedat the recent escalation of terrorist violence in Afghanistan, which demonstrates that safe havens and support systems continue to be available to the terrorists from across the border.

May 12, 2016, https://thewire.in/84672/pakistan-isis-afghanistan-russia/

32 Solovyov, Dmitry. "Russia's Interests Coincide with Taliban's in Fight against ISIS:..." Reuters. December 23, 2015. Accessed September 05, 2018. https://www.reuters.com/article/us-mideast-crisis-russia-taliban-idUSKBN0U61EQ20151223.

33 "RM's Address at 'VII Moscow Conference on International Security'." Year End Review 2017 –MNRE. April 05, 2018. Accessed August 29, 2018. http://pib.nic.in/PressReleaseIframePage.aspx?PRID=1527823

India has been a victim of terrorist attacks in the past. Recently, six Indians were among the seven people who have been abducted by unidentified armed men from Baghlan province in Afghanistan. On 6 June 2017, a Taliban rocket hit the Kabul home of India's top envoy to Afghanistan, fueling security concerns[34]. Attacks on Indians are construed in India as an attack on the bilateral relations. After 2009 attack on Indian mission in Kabul, then Foreign Secretary Nirupama Rao had said that Indo-Afghan relations are impermeable to such attacks and India has "unwavering commitment to pursue our bilateral development partnership and assist the people of Afghanistan in realising a democratic, peaceful and prosperous Afghanistan[35]." The Indian mission, consulates and about 150 personnel working on various projects are vulnerable to Taliban attacks. Pakistan is wary of India's growing footprint in Afghanistan and is trying to offset it with strengthening its strategic depth in Afghanistan through its proxies. Lt Gen Vincent Stewart, Director, US Defence Intelligence, during a hearing on Afghanistan at the Senate Armed Services Committee in 2017 stated, "They (Pakistan) view all of the challenges through the lens of an Indian threat to the state of Pakistan. So they hold in reserve terrorist organisations. So that — if Afghanistan leans towards India, they will no longer be supportive of an idea of a stable and secure Afghanistan that could undermine Pakistan interests.[36]"

India's strategic interests in Afghanistan devolve around access to Central Asia, economic interests and energy security. Therefore, a stable Afghanistan is vital for early operationalisation of Chahbahar -Saranj-Delaram axis, INSTC via Iran and Turkmenistan-

---

34 Totakhil, Habib Khan, and Jessica Donati. "Taliban Rocket Hits India Compound in Kabul." The Wall Street Journal. June 06, 2017. Accessed September 05, 2018. https://www.wsj.com/articles/afghan-peace-conference-begins-in-kabul-as-rocket-hits-indian-envoys-house-1496760668.

35 "Nirupama: Bid to Undermine Delhi-Kabul Friendship." The Hindu. December 16, 2016. Accessed August 28, 2018. https://www.thehindu.com/news/national/Nirupama-bid-to-undermine-Delhi-Kabul-friendship/article16885961.ece.

36 Anwar. "Pakistan Fears Indian Influence in Afghanistan, Say US Spy Chiefs." The Dawn. June 21, 2017. https://www.dawn.com/news/1335988

Afghanistan-Pakistan-India (TAPI) gas pipeline. On 23 February, during the inauguration of the TAPI pipeline in Herat in Afghanistan, Indian Minister of State for External Affairs (MoS MJ Akbar raised India's security concern. [37]

India, besides threat of terrorism is facing an inimical geopolitical alignment in Afghanistan, wherein, the interests of Russia – China – Iran and Pakistan coincide vis a vis India and the US. These countries are hobnobbing with the Taliban, whereas, India believes that such an approach is only emboldens it. It is worrisome that the new US sanctions on Iran could slow or even bring India's plan to develop berths at the Shahid Beheshti port in Chabahar to a halt, thereby impacting India's connectivity with Afghanistan. The new U.S. National Security Adviser, John Bolton, has a much tougher line on Iran and any further restrictions placed will make India's Chabahar plans more expensive and even unviable.[38] India needs a comprehensive policy dictated by its interests in terms of protecting its projects and carving out a larger regional role in the long-term stability of Afghanistan. India needs to consider long-term scenarios of its political, diplomatic and military options. For a larger regional role, it can work diplomatically towards the creation of a "concert of powers" - a regional grouping including the U.S., Russia, the EU, India, Iran, Central Asian Republics and China[39].

37 "Speech of MoS MJ Akbar at Inauguration Ceremony for Construction of TAPI Pipeline in Afghanistan.» Ministry of External Affairs, Government of India. February 24, 2018. Accessed August 29, 2018. http://www.mea.gov.in/ Speeches-Statements.htm?dtl/29515/Speech of MOS MJ Akbar at Inauguration Ceremony for Construction of TAPI pipeline in Afghanistan Herat February 23 2018. http://www.mea.gov.in/Speeches-Statements.htm?dtl/29515/Speech +of+MOS+MJ+Akbar+at+Inauguration+Ceremony+for+Construction+of+T API+pipeline+in+Afghanistan+Herat+February+23+2018

38 Haidar, Suhasini. "5 Ways India Could Be Affected by U.S. Decision to Pull out of Iran Nuclear Deal." The Hindu. May 09, 2018. Accessed August 29, 2018. https://www.thehindu.com/news/national/5-ways-india-could-be-affected-by- the-us-decision-to-withdraw-from-iran-nuclear-deal/article23820123.ece

39 D'Sousa, Shanthie Mariet. "Securing India's Interests in Afghanistan." The Hindu. December 16, 2016. Accessed August 28, 2018. https://www. thehindu.com/opinion/lead/Securing-Indiarsquos-interests-in-Afghanistan/ article16888279.ece.

Implications for Central Asian States. Geopolitically, Afghanistan and Central Asia form a part of the same strategic space. Afghanistan and the three Central Asian countries (Tajikistan, Uzbekistan and Turkmenistan) share rugged and porous borders and more than 50 per cent of Afghanistan's ethnicities are of Central Asian origin (Tajiks, Hasaras, Uzbeks and Turkmen).

During the early nineties the fighters of Islamic Renaissance Party of Tajikistan and from late nineties Islamic Movement of Uzbekistan, Uighur fighters (ETIM) and Chechens have used the territory of Afghanistan to wage militancy in Central Asia, Xinjiang and Caucasus. Presently, Northern Afghanistan is being used by Non – Pashtun Taliban and ISKP to spread militancy in the region. Since 2016, Kazakhstan alone has witnessed about 33 terrorist related incidents. Uighur militants had bombed the Chinese Embassy in Bishkek. As per New York based Soufan group there are hundreds of ISIS cadres hailing from Central Asia, determined to escalate violence in the region.

As per Stratfor report[40], during the year 2016, in the month of May, militants had reportedly killed 27 Turkmen conscripts on the country's border with Afghanistan. Meanwhile, rocket fire from Afghanistan's northern district of Kaldar was reported near the southern Uzbek city of Termez in early May the same year. And on June 1, 2016, Tajikistan reportedly thwarted militants who were attempting to enter the country from Afghanistan. In 26 Aug 2018, armed militants and Tajik foresters clashed near the Afghanistan border with Tajikistan, killing several people in Afghanistan's Takhar province. In Aug 13, Taliban militants overran an Afghan border police post just 25 miles from this border attack, killing 12 police officers and five civilians. Few weeks before Islamic State-had killed foreign cyclists - an American couple, a Swiss citisen and a Dutch national - were killed; and the others - one Swiss, one Dutch, and one French- were injured. [41]

---

40 Afghanistan: Border Clashes Raise Concerns of Spreading Instability, www.stratfor.com, August 27, 2018. Accessed on August 29, 2018 from https://worldview.stratfor.com/article/afghanistan-border-clashes-raise-concerns-spreading-instability

41 Ibid .

Uzbekistan's Positive Role. President Shavkat Mirziyoyev, has shown great visionary leadership by mending relations with the Central Asian neighbors and boosting ties with Afghanistan. As per the Diplomat, Uzbekistan is playing a laudable role in peacebuilding in Afghanistan [42]

On 27 Mar 2018, Tashkent hosted a conference to discuss the Afghanistan conundrum. From August 7 to 10, a delegation of Taliban led by Sher Mohammad Abbas Staniksai, the Taliban's Qatar-based political chief, traveled to Uzbekistan[43]. As per reports the sides discussed Taliban's demands of withdrawal of international forces from Afghanistan and Uzbek role in development projects in Afghanistan.

Tashkent has renewed its energy behind mutually beneficial projects, in particular expanding existing rail links from Afghan-Uzbek border toward Iran through Herat and boosting the electricity trade.[44] In 2011, Uzbekistan completed an Asian Development Bank project to extend its rail line from the Termez to Mazar-i-Sharif. Tashkent recently pledged $500 million for the construction of the $1.8 billion, 657 km rail line from Mazar-i-Sharif to Herat .In 2009, Uzbekistan had commissioned a 150 megawatt electric transmission line from Tashkent to Kabul, and in March 2018 it announced it would soon start work on the 260-kilometer Surkhan-Pul-e-Khumri line to increase electricity exports to Afghanistan by 70 percent. Just for good measure, President Mirziyoyev ordered that the rate for electricity deliveries to Afghanistan be dropped from $0.076 to $0.05 per kilowatt.

During Ghani's first visit to Tashkent in December 2017, the

42 Durso, James. "Central Asia Opens the Door to Afghanistan." The Diplomat. May 18, 2018. Accessed September 05, 2018. https://thediplomat.com/2018/05/central-asia-opens-the-door-to-afghanistan/.

43 Khan, Tahir. "Afghan Taliban Hold Talks in Uzbekistan to Discuss Peace Prospects." Daily Times. August 12, 2018. Accessed September 05, 2018. https://dailytimes.com.pk/282008/afghan-taliban-hold-talks-in-uzbekistan-to-discuss-peace-prospects/.

44 Catherine Putz, Taliban Talks in Uzbekistan, Violence Continues in Afghanistan, www.Diplomat.com, 15 Aug 2018.

governments confirmed 20 bilateral agreements in numerous areas, such as protection of the Termez–Hairatan bridge (the "Friendship Bridge"), the implementation of the Mazar-i-Sharif–Herat railway line, the implementation of the construction of the Surkhan-Pul-e-Khumri power transmission line, legal assistance in civil, family and criminal cases, mutual assistance in customs matters, and cooperation in customs, agriculture, higher education, and air traffic control. The Afghan and Uzbek business communities followed suit by signing $500 million in contracts.

Role of India in Afghanistan

India and Afghanistan share strong historical and cultural ties since ancient period. India's engagement with Afghanistan is guided by Strategic Partnership Agreement of 2011, which is steered by a Council of Foreign Ministers. At the multi-lateral level India actively participates in deliberations at the SCO Contact Group on Afghanistan, Russia-India-China (RIC), BRICS, Heart of Asia Conference, Moscow format, Indo-Iran-Afghanistan trilateral agreement and India-US-Afghanistan trilateral dialogue and other international forums. At the 2nd meeting of SCO-Afghanistan Contact Group in Beijing held on 28 May 2018, India extended firm support to the Afghan led reconciliation process and role of SCO in peace building.[45] India has agreed to undertake joint projects with Russia[46] and China[47] in Afghanistan. The Pentagon report titled 'Enhancing Security and Stability in Afghanistan' underlined that "India is Afghanistan's most reliable regional partner and the largest

---

45 "Second SCO- Afghanistan Contact Group Meeting, Beijing." Ministry of External Affairs, Government of India. May 28, 2018. Accessed August 24, 2018. https://www.mea.gov.in/press-releases.htm?dtl/29926/second+sco+afghanistan+contact+group+meeting+beijing+may+28+2018

46 "Informal Summit between India and Russia." Year End Review 2017 –MNRE. May 21, 2018. Accessed August 24, 2018. http://pib.nic.in/PressReleaseIframePage.aspx?PRID=1532998

47 "MEA | E-citisen/RTI : Parliament Q & A : Rajya Sabha." Ministry of External Affairs, Government of India. August 09, 2018. Accessed August 29, 2018. https://mea.gov.in/rajya-sabha.htm?dtl/30305/QUESTION_NO2580_SPECIAL_PROJECT_IN_AFGHANISTAN

contributor of development assistance in the region."[48] India can leverage its rich experience in combating terrorism by exchanging data with the SCO and share its expertise during the counter terrorism exercises.[49]

India has invested \$2 billion for civil capacity building, such as, construction of Salma dam, roads, power lines, parliament building and telecommunication infrastructure. Assistance is provided by way of developing TV industry, agriculture sector, irrigation, health, transport and grant of gratis vacancies to Afghan students in academic institutions in India.Liberal medical visasare being issued for Afghans for the treatment in Indian hospitals. According to the figures of the Ministry of Tourism, the inflow of medical tourists coming from Afghanistan increased in 2017 and has reached to 55,681.[50] India is fast turning out to be most affordable medical destination for Afghans.

India has successfully completed the Phases I and II of the Small Development Projects (SDP) scheme designed for border districts of Afghanistan.[51] The inauguration of the Dedicated Air Cargo Corridor in June 2017 between Kabul-Delhi and Kandahar-Delhi has provided a fresh impetus to bilateral trade.[52] Apart from Kabul, two more cities – Mazar-e-Sharif and Herat wereconnected to New

48 "India Most Reliable Regional Partner of Afghanistan: Pentagon." The Economic Times. July 12, 2018. Accessed August 24, 2018. https://economictimes.indiatimes.com/news/defence/india-most-reliable-regional-partner-of-afghanistan-pentagon/articleshow/62089212.cms

49 "Informal Summit between India and Russia." Year End Review 2017 –MNRE. May 21, 2018. Accessed August 24, 2018. http://pib.nic.in/PressReleaseIframePage.aspx?PRID=1532998

50 Kumar, Navtan. "Over 50per cent Medical Tourists to India Are from Bangladesh." The Sunday Guardian Live. August 04, 2018. https://www.sundayguardianlive.com/news/50-medical-tourists-india-bangladesh

51 "MoU for 5 Small Development Projects (SDP) Signed." Embassy /High Commission /Consulate General of India. January 10, 2015. Accessed August 29, 2018. https://eoi.gov.in/kabul/?3810?000

52 "India-Afghanistan Relations." Ministry of External Affairs, Government of India. May 28, 2018. Accessed August 24, 2018. https://www.mea.gov.in/Portal/ForeignRelation/1Afghanistan_October_2017.pdf

Delhi by air in October 2017.[53] India also operationalised Chabahar port for supply of grains and other products through Saranj-Delaram axis. During the second meeting of India-Afghanistan Joint Working Group on Development Cooperation (JWG-DC) on August 9, 2018, the Afghan side appreciated India's timely assistance of 170,000 tonnes of wheat and 2,000 tonnes of pulses at a time when large parts of the country are suffering from drought.[54] This assignment was a part of the one million tonnes of food grains sent to Afghanistan. In order to give further impetus to multi-modal connectivity, India has agreed to build a 500-km railroad from Chabahar to Zahedan, the provincial capital of Sistan-Baluchistan, close to the Afghan border.[55] Under the enhanced India-Afghanistan-US partnership, India has commenced organising "Passage to Prosperity", the India-Afghanistan Trade and Investment Show, supported by USAID, from 2017. [56] The 2017, the Indo - US - Afghan trade and investment show in Delhi attended by 200 Afghan, and 800 Indian businessmen. This year's Investment show is scheduled to take place in Mumbai from September 12 to 15.

Under thenext generation 'New Development Partnership,' India has pledged $ 1 billion aid to Kabul for construction of 116

---

53 Roche, Elizabeth. "Now, Flights from New Delhi to Two More Afghan Cities." Https://www.livemint.com/. October 02, 2017. Accessed August 29, 2018 https://www.livemint.com/Politics/9ycJI01C5uyeqJciwnlSuO/Now-flights-from-New-Delhi-to-two-more-Afghan-cities.html

54 "Second Meeting of India-Afghanistan Joint Working Group on Development Cooperation (JWG-DC) in Kabul." Ministry of External Affairs, Government of India. August 10, 2018. Accessed August 29, 2018. https://www.mea.gov.in/press-releases.htm?dtl/30310/second+meeting+of+indiaafghanistan+joint+working+group+on+development+cooperation+jwgdc+in+kabul

55 "India, Iran Welcome Lease Contract for Chabahar Port Operations." Business Standard. February 17, 2018. Accessed August 29, 2018. https://www.business-standard.com/article/news-ani/india-iran-welcome-lease-contract-for-chabahar-port-operations-118021700639_1.html

56 "Economic Bonds between India and Afghanistan to Strengthen through the Trade and Investment Show." U.S. Agency for International Development. September 27, 2017. Accessed August 29, 2018. https://www.usaid.gov/afghanistan/news-information/press-releases/Sept-27-2017-India-Afghanistan-Trade-and-Investment-Show

high- impact community development projects to be implemented in 31 provinces[57]. In addition, six new projects in low cost housing for returning Afghan refugees in Nangarhar province, road connectivity (to Band e Amir in Bamyan province), national park, economic development, water supply schemes (Shahtoot Dam and water supply for Kabul and Charikar city in Parwan province), establishment of gypsum board manufacturing plant in Kabul, construction of polyclinic in Mazar-e-Sharif are being undertaken.[58] Some of the ongoing projects India have undertaken are the development of communication infrastructure (optic fibre) and the Surobi 2 hydropower plant with capacity of 180 MW[59]. Many Indian companies are doing business in Afghanistan, mostly in the power sector. KEC (electrical transmission lines), Phoenix (consultancy in electrical transmission), AIPL (establishment of hydropower project in Helmand province), Gammon India (power transmission line & power sub-stations), KPTL (power transmission line) are some of the major companies. Besides, the aviation firm Spice Jet is also active in Afghanistan[60].

The Union Cabinet has approved the signing of a Cooperation Arrangement between Food Safety & Standards Authority of India (FSSAI), Ministry of Health & Family Welfare (MoH&FW) and Ministry of Agriculture, Irrigation & Livestock (MAIL), Afghanistan for cooperation in the field of Food Safety and related areas. The cooperation arrangement will facilitate information sharing training and capacity building measure and learning from each other's best

57 "India Announces Taking up 116 High-impact Projects in Afghanistan - Times of India." The Times of India. September 21, 2017. Accessed September 05, 2018. https://timesofindia.indiatimes.com/india/india-announces-taking-up-116-high-impact-projects-in-afghanistan/articleshow/60783744.cms.

58 Haidar, Suhasini. "India to Further Aid Afghan Troops." The Hindu. September 11, 2017. Accessed August 29, 2018. https://www.thehindu.com/news/international/india-to-further-aid-afghan-troops/article19660585.ece

59 Roy, Shubhajit. "From Infrastructure to Education, India's $2-billion Role in Afghanistan." The Indian Express. May 07, 2018. Accessed September 05, 2018. https://indianexpress.com/article/india/infrastructure-to-education-indias-2-billion-role-in-afghanistan-5166145/.

60 Ibid

practice to improve food safety ecosystem.[61] During the 2nd Strategic Partnership meet, the two countries had also signed Motor Vehicles Agreement for the Regulation of Passenger, Personal and Cargo Vehicular Traffic.

An MoU was signed for mutual cooperation in the field of pharmaceutical products regulation, and the Orbit Frequency Coordination Agreement was signed between India and Afghanistan on South Asia Satellite (SAS)[62].

India announced several capacity building scholarships for neighbouring countries including Afghanistan during the Science and Technology (S&T) Ministers Conclave at India International Science Festival (IISF) 2017, Chennai. The 2018-India Science and Research Fellowship (ISRF) scheme will provide a fully paid fellowship to researchers, scientists and academicians from Afghanistan for human capacity building in S&T.[63] Afghan National Agriculture Sciences and Technology University (ANASTU) was established with Indian government's financial & technical assistance; similarly, on the request by the Afghanistan government, India is providing technical and financial assistance for the establishment of Afghan Mining Institute in Kabul. After reconstruction of the Habibia High School, Kabul at a cost of $5.1 million, India has been supporting the school by way of upgradation of facilities, training of teachers. Besides these government-funded projects, Aptech, a private firm, is providing IT training for Afghan youth in the country.

61 "Cabinet Approvesa Cooperation Arrangement between India and Afghanistan for Cooperation in the Field of Food Safety and Related Areas." Year End Review 2017 –MNRE. April 04, 2018. Accessed August 29, 2018. http://pib.nic.in/newsite/erelcontent.aspx?relid=178406

62 "MEA | Statements : Bilateral/Multilateral Documents." Ministry of External Affairs, Government of India. Accessed September 05, 2018. https://mea.gov.in/bilateral-documents.htm?dtl/28936/Joint_Statement_on_the_2nd_Strategic_Partnership_Council_Meeting_between_India_and_Afghanistan_New_Delhi_September_11_2017.

63 "India Announces Several Capacity Building Scholarships For Neighbouring Countries." Year End Review 2017 –MNRE. October 13, 2017. Accessed August 29, 2018. http://pib.nic.in/newsite/erelcontent.aspx?relid=171701

In terms of security assistance, India has supplied non-lethal military equipment, four helicopter gunships, and based on the request from Afghanistan is providing repair of MI 35 helicopters, while supply of transport planes and supply of other military hardware is under consideration. About 1000 military personnel and a fair number of civil servants, policemen and other specialists are being trained in India. 100 beds are earmarked for battle causalities in multi-specialty military hospitals. India will also provide 500 scholarships for graduate studies in India for the next of kin of ANSF martyrs for the academic year 2018-2019 to honor their sacrifices "for the cause of entire humanity" and ensuring the safety of Indians working in Afghanistan. Additionally, the Union Cabinet chaired by the Prime Minister has given its approval for signing an MoU between India and Afghanistan on Technical Cooperation on Police Training and Development. It will help in capacity building of Afghanistan National Police and improving the security apparatus in the region.[64]

India – Uzbekistan Convergence in Afghanistan

At the international conference on Afghanistan held in Tashkent on 27 March 2018, the remarks of[65] India's MoS External Affairs M J Akbar at the conference reflect convergence in India - Uzbekistan views on Afghanistan, as encapsulated in the joint declaration , "We recognise that a political settlement that is Afghan-led and Afghan-owned, supported by close regional counterterrorism and counter-narcotics cooperation, and regional economic cooperation and connectivity are key to the peace and prosperity of Afghanistan and the entire region"[66]. The Tashkent Declaration further underscored

64 "Cabinet Approves Bilateral MoU between India and Afghanistan on Technical Cooperation on Police Training and Development." Year End Review 2017 –MNRE. September 27, 2017. Accessed August 29, 2018. http://pib.nic.in/newsite/PrintRelease.aspx?relid=171158

65 Dipanjan Roy Chaudhury, Tashkent echoes India's stand on Afghan peace process, Economic Times, 28 march , 2018. Accessed on August 29 from https://economictimes.indiatimes.com/news/defence/tashkent-echoes-indias-stand-on-afghan-peace/articleshow/63497108.cms

66 "Declaration of the Tashkent Conference on Afghanistan: Peace Process, Security Cooperation and Regional Connectivity." Uzbekistan National

respect for sovereignty and territorial integrity of Afghanistan, and non-interference in its internal affairs and condemned terrorism attacks in all its forms and manifestations.Uzbekistan president Shavkat Mirziyoyev said the fight against terrorism was a common challenge for the region, whereas, MJ Akbar asserted that both India and Afghanistan were victims ofcross-border terrorism and ideological extremism and brutal terrorism, often sponsored from beyond their borders.

Conclusion

India seeks a stable, prosperous Afghanistan that is fully integrated with global trading network-an Afghanistan that will not become a breeding ground of trans- national like terrorism; Afghan people have strength, wisdom, courage and perseverance to start a new and peaceful life for the sake of prosperity of their children and future generations. India is against zero sum mentality and do not favour Afghanistan being used as a chessboard for proxy conflicts. India strongly favours that the neighbouring countries and the international community at large should join hands in defeating terrorism and supporting Afghan owned Afghan led peace process for global peace and security. India has live operational experience in combating cross-border terrorism and undertaking civic action programmes with Afghan characteristics. India and Uzbekistan therefore can be a partners of choice in peace building in Afghanistan, be it part of the UN, SCO or any other multilateral mechanism that is based on a win – win paradigm.

News Agency. Accessed September 05, 2018. http://usa.uz/en/politics/declaration-of-the-tashkent-conference-on-afghanistan-peace--28-03-2018?month=02&year=2018&ELEMENT_CODE=declaration-of-the-tashkent-conference-on-afghanistan-peace--28-03-2018&SECTION_CODE=politics.

SECTION – III

Prospects for Cooperation on Regional Connectivity, Trade and Transit between India and Uzbekistan – Uzbekistan's View

Rustam Makhmudov

Introduction

The Central Asian region and India have significant potential for developing mutual trade, economic and investment ties. However, it is still far from being fully implemented. One of the main reasons for this lies in the transport and communication sector. Central Asia is located in the Eurasia hinterland with no direct access to the ports of the Indian Ocean. Moreover, a serious deterrent in the development of a number of transport corridors to the southern direction is the ongoing conflict in Afghanistan and the traditionally difficult relations between India and Pakistan. Nevertheless, despite the existing difficulties, the cooperation in the field of creating new communication routes has promising prospects.

In terms of the development of connectivity in the framework of interstate cooperation, the first point which is traditionally considered is the ability of partner countries to fill existing and potential automobile and railway corridors, ports with capacity to handle the cargoes over the near to medium term. This entails a comprehensive analysis of the strategies and objectives of the national economic development of partner countries, the level of their integration into regional and global trade, investment and financial ties, value-added chains, etc. The outcomes depends upon the target areas in which governments and business circles are planning to invest and identifications of the points of convergences based on which the projects for joint transport and communication corridors can be arrived at to facilitate in increasing the turnover of joint economic projects.

Regarding the prospects for connectivity between Central Asia and India, based on the above criteria, the increase in Central Asian-Indian economic development would serve as the basis for identifying the main points of convergences of interests.

New regional policy of Uzbekistan as an incentive for the development of the whole Central Asia

Central Asia as a region is on the verge of reaching rapid economic growth; the new policy of Uzbekistan plays a crucial role in this regard. The development of Uzbekistan's political, economic, cultural and humanitarian ties with Kazakhstan and Turkmenistan, as well as the rapid restoration of good relationship with Kyrgyzstan and Tajikistan has a qualitatively impact on the course of development of the entire region.

This is a stark improvement to the situation prevailed earlier. Then many experts had opined that due to lack of intra-regional trade and economic interdependence, the region appeared to be disintegrating as each country was drifting towards extra regional markets. All this was also superimposed with a very complex web of problems, many of which were formed back in the 90s of the last century; and the pessimists believed it would not be possible to resolve them. However, the new regional course of President Shavkat Mirziyoyev has showed that the pessimists were wrong and most of the old problems were not so complicated. In reality in all countries of the region came forward for strengthening the entire spectrum of interstate and international relations.

The removal of many barriers to trade, to the flows of people and capital between Uzbekistan and its neighbors caused a rapid, and in some cases positive growth in trade. In 2016, trade with Tajikistan grew 5.7 times as compared to 2015 or up to $69.2 million.[1] In

---

1 Товарооборот между Узбекистаном и Таджикистаном вырос на 85 per cent. 20.12.2017. http://kommersant.uz/news/tovarooborot-mezhdu-uzbekistanom-i-tadzhikistanom-vyros-na-85

2017, these dynamics remained, which indicated the growth of trade turnover to $240 million.[2] If such growth rates continue, Uzbekistan will be able to catch up with Dushanbe's leading foreign trade partners – Russia ($843 million) and Kazakhstan ($754 million). As Shavkat Mirziyeyev's visit to Tajikistan on March 9-10, 2018 showed, both countries intend to bring the mutual trade to $500 million in the coming years.

A similar situation was observed in the Uzbek-Kyrgyz trade turnover, which in January-September 2017 increased by 60 per cent compared with the same period of 2016 or from $140 million to $231 million.[3] The parties also set a goal to increase it to $500 million in the short term, which is quite feasible, given the fact that in 2017 representatives of business circles of Uzbekistan and Kyrgyzstan signed agreements and contracts for more than $600 million.[4] Good prospects for the growth of trade occurred between Uzbekistan and Kazakhstan – the third leading trade partner of Uzbekistan after China and Russia. It is expected that the implementation of agreements reached in 2017 at two Uzbek-Kazakh business forums in Astana and Tashkent for the amount of $1.2 billion would lead to the increase of mutual trade from $2 billion to $5 billion by 2020.[5]

Thus, this new policy coupled with reciprocal desire for rapprochement amongst all the neighbors, could lead Central Asia towards an integrated economy. Moreover Uzbekistan and its regional partners have started laying a new foundation, which should contribute positively towards long-term economic growth for the region. Herein, three factors merit consideration, as mentioned below.

---

2   Мирзиёев пригласил Рахмона в Узбекистан. Пресс-служба президента Узбекистана. 09.03.2018. https: //ru.sputniknews-uz.com/ politics/20180309/7676182/Mirzieev-Rahmon-priglashenie.html

3   Товарооборот Узбекистана с Кыргызстаном вырос на 60 per cent. http:// kommersant.uz/news/tovarooborot-uzbekistana-s-kyrgyzstanom-vyros-na-60

4   Товарооборот Узбекистана с Кыргызстаном вырос на 60 per cent. http:// kommersant.uz/news/tovarooborot-uzbekistana-s-kyrgyzstanom-vyros-na-60

5   Узбекистан и Казахстан подписали соглашения на $1,2 млрд. 18 сентября 2017, https://www.gaseta.uz/ru/2017/09/18/business-forum/

First, large-scale domestic reforms in Uzbekistan aimed at liberalisation of the monetary and financial system, improvement of the business environment for national and foreign entrepreneurs, investors and exporters with the provision of numerous benefits, the creation of free economic zones and a tough fight against corruption. It should be emphasised that Uzbekistan strives to obtain a sovereign credit rating and launch a Eurobond issue, which is illustrated on a memorandum signed with the American "Citigroup" that will undertake the preparation of the corresponding "road map".[6] In Central Asia, only Kazakhstan and Kyrgyzstan have sovereign credit ratings. All efforts undertaken by Uzbekistan would create new incentives for the growth of its economy, which will have a positive impact on the region. The increase in the capacity of the Uzbek consumer market will automatically become a catalyst for growth for those industries and segments of industry, agriculture and services of neighboring countries, whose exports are oriented to Uzbekistan.

Second is the policy of embedding the processes for the Fourth Industrial Revolution (4IR). The programs oriented towards 4IR are being implemented in Uzbekistan and Kazakhstan. "Mirzo Ulugbek Innovation Centre" was established in April 2017 in Tashkent, and several high-tech facilities are being built on the basis of "smart city". A "Tech Garden" has been operating in Almaty for several years, which has become a centre for the generation of new technologies and knowledge for the Kazakh economy. In both countries, much work is also being done to create an energy grid based on renewable energy sources, based on the use of solar and wind energy. In future these would lead to new types of high technology products with highly added value, create an environmentally friendly and energy-efficient economy and, in general, an economic system based on the principles of sustainable development.

Third is the creation of the most extensive and competitive intra-regional transport communication system. Over the past year, several breakthroughs were witnessed. First, the start of cargo

---

6 Узбекистан готовится к первому размещению евробондов. https://www.gaseta.uz/ru/2018/02/22/eurobonds/

shipment along the "Andijan-Osh-Irkeshtam-Kashgar" road. In October 2017 cargo from Tashkent through Kyrgyzstan to China's Kashgar (900 km) was delivered in just two days at an average speed of 50-60 km/h.[7]

The resumption of the tripartite working group on the construction of the railway "Uzbekistan - Kyrgyzstan - China" is considered to be major breakthrough. At a meeting of the project participants held in Tashkent in December 2017, a phased schedule was set for 2018, the results of the initial survey for this route was to be presented in April, the feasibility study in August, and by the end of the year a finance model is to be presented.[8]

The restoration of the railway line "Galaba-Amusang" is another breakthrough. It connects the Khatlon region of Tajikistan with the Uzbek railway grid. It was operationalised during the state visit of Shavkat Mirziyoyev to Tajikistan on March 9-10 this year. This will increase the level of economic activity in the south-western regions of Tajikistan and strengthen their foreign trade, which will be facilitated by discounts being provided by Uzbekistan for goods that are imported by Tajikistan on this route. A 40 per cent discount for import on the Keles-Kudukli railway route and 30-50 percent discounts for petroleum products and other goods on the Karakalpakstan-Kudukli route.[9] These discounts have already seen a drop in prices for some consumer goods in the Tajik market, such as flour.

The revitalising influence on the development of transport and trade connectivity within Central Asia could be further facilitated by the simplification of transit procedures for a number of goods

7 АВТОКОЛОННА "ТАШКЕНТ-КАШГАР" УСПЕШНО ПРИБЫЛА В КОНЕЧНЫЙ ПУНКТ НАЗНАЧЕНИЯ. http://jahonnews.uz/ru/aktualno/124/40767/

8 Точный маршрут ж/д Китай — Кыргызстан — Узбекистан будет готов к апрелю. http://ru.sputniknews-uz.com/economy/20171227/7166716/tochnyj-marshrut-zh-d-kitaj-kyrgyzstan-uzbekistan-budet-gotov-k-aprelyu.html

9 Узбекистан вновь предоставил скидки Таджикистану на транзит железнодорожных грузов. http://avesta.tj/2018/01/18/uzbekistan-vnov-predostavil-skidki-tadzhikistanu-na-tranzit-zheleznodorozhnyh-gruzov/

through the territory of Uzbekistan. From March 1, 2018, the procedure for issuing permission by the Cabinet of Ministers of Uzbekistan to transit through the territory of the republic for taxable goods by road and rail has been canceled.[10]

The freight turnover with Kazakhstan is also increasing. In 2017, the volume increased by 8 per cent and amounted to more than 20.5 million tons. For the first two months of 2018, traffic volumes increased by 44 per cent compared to the same period of 2017.[11] If such rates continue, it is likely that in the coming years the need for expanding the capacity of railways and building new highways between Uzbekistan and Kazakhstan will become reality. The necessity would also grow when the countries achieve the goal of increasing bilateral trade to $5 billion.

A promising project to further improve trade could be the construction of the railway line "Uchkuduk-Kyzylorda", which would connect the central regions of the two countries. The idea was proposed by the Ambassador of Kazakhstan in Uzbekistan Yerik Utembayev in December 2016 during his working trip to Navoi region of Uzbekistan.[12] The issue of increasing the route capacity of the roads linking Uzbekistan and Kazakhstan would contribute to the growing volumes of their trade that transit through Uzbek and Kazakh territory to third countries such as Afghanistan, Tajikistan, Russia, China, the South Caucasus, Turkey and the European Union.

In addition to the efforts of the Central Asian nations to develop railways and highways, Kazakhstan is developing its ports on the Caspian Sea - Aktau and Kuryk, which are connected to the Central Asian railway network. In Aktau, extension work of the port's capacity has been completed. Currently, the port is capable of handling 3.2 million tons of dry cargo and 12.5 million tons of

---

10 Упрощен транзит подакцизной продукции через Узбекистан. 2 марта 2018. https://www.gaseta.uz/ru/2018/03/02/goods/

11 Узбекистан и Казахстан увеличат товарооборот до $5 млрд к 2020 году. https://www.gaseta.uz/ru/2018/03/15/comission/

12 Узбекистан и Казахстан планируют построить новую железную дорогу. https://ru.sputnik-tj.com/asia/20161209/1021271590.html

crude oil per year. The capacity of the Kuryk port by the end of 2017 was brought to 1.5 million tons of dry cargo per year. After the completion of the construction of two railway and two automobile piers, the port's throughput capacity will be 6 million tons of cargo and 20,000 cars per year.[13] These ports will allow diversifying the output of Central Asian countries to the world markets.

In addition, it should be noted that it is not feasible to create a sustainable growth for the economies of Central Asia without development of trade, industry, investment, scientific, technological and tourist ties with the global markets. There are several such markets in the immediate vicinity of Central Asia, India, which has the world's third largest based on GDP at purchasing power parity (9.49 trillion dollars) and the sixth largest in nominal GDP (2.45 trillion dollars).[14]

India becomes one of the drivers of the development of the world economy

Unfortunately, the current scale of trade and economic relations between Central Asian countries and India continues to be relatively low. One of the main reasons for this is the lack of connectivity and trade access to each other's markets.

However, though the trade turnover between Uzbekistan and India has doubled since 2011, it amounted to only $370 million in 2016.[15] Kazakhstan-India trade is also relatively low - $618.4 million in 2016, the highest – $1.3 billion in 2014. The trade between Kazakhstan with India is based on four sectors. Of the Kazakhstan's exports, 47.1 per cent fall on uranium supplies and 43.7 per cent is

---

13 Ольга Золотых, Ренат Дусалиев. «В порту Курык завершилось строительство автомобильного паромного комплекса». http://khabar. kz/ru/news/obshchestvo/item/98190-v-portu-kuryk-savershilos-stroitelstvo-avtomobilnogo-paromnogo-kompleksa

14 The World's Top 10 Economies By Prableen Bajpai, CFA (ICFAI). July 7, 2017. https://www.investopedia.com/articles/investing/022415/worlds-top-10-economies.asp#ixzz59nXnvGjH

15 Узбекистан и Индия подписали контракты и соглашения на $150 млн. 24 августа 2017. https://www.gaseta.uz/ru/2017/08/24/india/

oil, and the major Indian exports to Kazakhstan are drugs (27.6 per cent) and tea (19.1 per cent) .[16]

There was a fall in trade volumes between Turkmenistan and India. In the fiscal year 2016-2017, it amounted to only $79.07 million (India – $57.75 million, Turkmenistan – $ 21.32 million), falling from $109 million in 2016-2017. The main Indian exports to Turkmenistan are the products LG (South Korean), cars, woollen clothes, pharmaceutical, frozen meat and tyres. The Turkmen exports to India are dominated by raw skins and products of inorganic chemistry.[17]

India accounts for only 0.5 per cent of Kyrgyzstan's export. Trade is mainly carried out by small entrepreneurs, which is why it is subject to serious fluctuations. Due to this the Kyrgyz exports to India in some years showed a decline of 15.2 times. The structure of bilateral trade is also very limited; it consists of mainly oil products and bitumen minerals from Kyrgyzstan ($483,000) and medicines ($14 million), mechanical appliances ($1.5 million) and clothing ($1,18 million) from India.[18]

The trade turnover between Tajikistan and India too remains insignificant. In the fiscal year 2016-2017, Indian companies supplied pharmaceutical and food products, clothing and accessories, iron and steel products to Tajikistan accounting $20.51 million. This is below the highest level of exports to Tajikistan achieved in 2013-2014 ($54.27 million). In turn, Tajik exports demonstrated a recovery, after it fell to $860 thousand in 2013-2014, from $23.02 million in 2010-2011. In 2016-2017, deliveries of various types of ore, aluminum, organic chemicals, dry fruit, vegetable oils and cotton from Tajikistan reached $21.82 million.[19]

---

16 Взаимная торговля Казахстана с Индией. http://www.export.gov.kz/public/ files/analytics/countryReview/references/2016/ per centD0 per cent98 per centD0 per centBD per centD0 per centB4 per centD0 per centB8 per centD1 per cent8F per cent202016.pdf

17 India-Turkmenistan Relations. http://www.eoi.gov.in/ashgabat/?0760?000

18 Атамбаев и Моди: Три причины сотрудничества. 19.12.2016. http://knews. kg/2016/12/atambaev-i-modi-tri-prichiny-sotrudnichestva/

19 India-Tajikistan Bilateral Relations. http://www.mea.gov.in/Portal/

There is thus a need for the countries of Central Asia and India to enhance their trade relations by diversifying the export products. The Central Asian countries need to closely examine the long-term trends of the Indian economy and look for convergences to build upon. It may be noted that the Indian economy is growing both quantitatively and qualitatively.

In the report of the OECD, post 2014 India became the fastest growing economy among all economies of the G20 with an average annual GDP growth of about 7.5 per cent.[20] Indian exports had crossed $100 billion in 2005-2006, and by 2013-2014 it had reached $314.4 billion.[21] The subsequent recession was caused due to the crisis in the world economy; however, by the end of 2018, the exports are expected to cross $300 billion.[22] It should be noted that 70 per cent of all exports are from five Indian states - Maharashtra, Gujarat, Tamil Nadu, Karnataka and Telangana.[23]

At the same time the import has also grown. In 2012-2013 it had reached $490.7 billion, $164 billion of which fell on oil imports and $326.7 billion on non-oil products.[24] This suggests that the Indian market is already one of the largest markets, can have an impact on the world prices for a large sector of goods, and also on the overall global economic growth. It is predicted that by 2025 India will

ForeignRelation/Tajikistan_August_2017.pdf

20 OECD Economic Surveys. India. February 2017. Overview. https://www.oecd.org/eco/surveys/INDIA-2017-OECD-economic-survey-overview.pdf

21 Reserve Bank of India. TABLE 126 : INDIA'S FOREIGN TRADE - US DOLLAR. https://rbidocs.rbi.org.in/rdocs/Publications/PDFs/TABLE126C84D3DEADFFB467181EF4B113D7D56B0.PDF

22 Exports up 12.3 per cent in December but imports jumped 21 per cent; trade deficit at its widest in 3 years. January 16, 2018. https://www.businesstoday.in/current/economy-politics/exports-up-12.3-per-cent-december-imports-jumped-21-per-cent-trade-deficit-widest-in-3-years/story/268126.html

23 India's external sector prospects look bright: Survey PTI | Jan 29, 2018. //economictimes.indiatimes.com/articleshow/62693190.cms?utm_source=contentofinterest&utm_medium=text&utm_campaign=cppst

24 Reserve Bank of India. TABLE 126 : INDIA'S FOREIGN TRADE - US DOLLAR. https://rbidocs.rbi.org.in/rdocs/Publications/PDFs/TABLE126C84D3DEADFFB467181EF4B113D7D56B0.PDF

become the 3rd largest consumer market in the world, which will allow Delhi to extract large dividends in the form of foreign direct investment in the production and innovation sector.

Hence it is natural that Delhi is a consistent supporter of "free trade". Prime Minister Narendra Modi at the World Economic Forum in Davos, Switzerland, in January 2018, stated that he considered protectionism to be one of the three most serious challenges for the modern world, along with climate change and terrorism.[25] This position coincides with the economic philosophy of Kazakhstan and Kyrgyzstan, which are already members of the WTO, as well as Uzbekistan, which declared its accession to the WTO to be one of the priorities of its foreign policy.[26]

In India, the flagship programme to give impetus to make India into a global manufacturing hub is the "Make in India" program, aimed at developing domestic production in 25 sectors of the economy with a focus on innovative development and taking into account the requirements of the Fourth Industrial Revolution. A promising area in this case may be cooperation between Central Asia and India in the field of renewable energy, since the Indian government has embarked on the implementation of the world's largest program for the construction of renewable energy facilities with a capacity of 175 Gigawatts by 2022.[27] Cooperation in the field of innovations too has good prospects. The Indian government supports the "Startup India" program and constantly increases spending on Research & Development, wherein, it was ranked 6th in the world. Also, India has 20 thousand start-ups that are already functioning and 4 new

---

25 PM Narendra Modi's Speech At World Economic Forum In Davos: Full Text. January 23, 2018. https://www.ndtv.com/india-news/pm-narendra-modis-speech-at-world-economic-forum-in-davos-full-text-1803790

26 Вступление в ВТО — один из приоритетов внешнеэкономической политики» — Жамшид Ходжаев.14 марта 2018. https://www.gaseta.uz/ru/2018/03/14/wto/

27 India to achieve 175 GW renewable energy ahead of 2022 deadline. Feb 23, 2018. //economictimes.indiatimes.com/articleshow/63046393.cms?utm_source=contentofinterest&utm_medium=text&utm_campaign=cppst

ones occur every day.[28]

New opportunities for cooperation of Central Asia and India can be in the field of information and biotechnology, electrical equipment, the defense sector, as well as agriculture and food industry. Considering that the population of India has already reached 1.22 billion people, and by 2020 1/3 of the country's population will live in cities, it will increase their purchasing power and increase the consumer demand for millions of these people. Similar trends are also being witnessed in the countries of Central Asia. The countries of Central Asia and India could consider cooperation in the creation of joint Mega Food Parks consisting of several components, such as the collection and delivery of farm products to processing centres, with the further delivery of finished goods to the domestic consumer market and for export. A similar project of 42 parks worth $2.38 billion is being implemented in India.[29]

India also has rich experience of cooperation with the world's leading corporations in the creation of supply value chains, and the countries of Central Asia could consider the possibility of cooperation with Delhi in such a segment of the global economy.

Ways to Overcome Barriers in Connectivity

Diversification trade is one of the aspects of improving the Indian-Central Asian trade and economic relations, but without the development of connectivity, it may not materialise. It is hence important to search for options for cooperation in this aspect for India and Central Asia.

Central Asia has a process in place for creating there is a fast process of creating new transport highways and removing barriers to the movement of goods. In turn, India is implementing a large-scale project "Sagarmala", worth $100 billion. This program provides for the modernisation of existing ports and the development of

28 ON THE PATH TO A NEW INDIA: 5 THINGS TO KNOW. http://www. makeinindia.com/five-things-to-know

29 Food Processing. Make in India. http://www.makeinindia.com/sector/food-processing

new ones; improvement of their connection with industries through optimisation of costs and time spent on transportation of goods; development in close proximity to the ports of industrial clusters; promotion of programs for the sustainable development of coastal areas.[30] The project "Sagarmala" would give a powerful stimulus to the development of foreign economic relations of India.

Based on geographic and the geopolitical scenario in South Asia, connectivity of Central Asia and India is currently possible only through the territory of Iran, which in turn is ready to become a link between the two, and is actively investing in the development of its own transport infrastructure.

For the future of Indian-Central Asian trade ties, the port of Chabahar on the coast of the Gulf of Oman is of particular interest. During the visit of Iranian President Hassan Roukhani to India in February 2018, an agreement was signed between the Iranian Port and Maritime Organisation and the Indian Ports Global Limited on the transfer of the port of Shahid Beheshti (Phase 1 port of Chabahar) under the operational control of India for a cost of the US $85 million. According to the joint statement of the leaders of the two countries, the Iranian side welcomed Indian investments in the construction of a plant for the production of fertilizers, petrochemical and metallurgical plants in the free trade zone Chabahar.[31] It is quite obvious that some of the future products from these plants can find their markets in the Central Asian countries.

This agreement means that Chabahar could actually become India's outpost to expand its trade links with central Asia and Afghanistan. Through the port, the first deliveries of Indian wheat were already made within the framework of humanitarian assistance to Afghanistan. Chabahar can also play a key role in India's participation in the Oman-Iran-Turkmenistan-Uzbekistan-

---

30 About SagarMala. Concept & Objectives. http://sagarmala.gov.in/about-sagarmala/vision-objectives

31 India-Iran Joint Statement during Visit of the President of Iran to India. February 17, 2018. http://www.mea.gov.in/bilateral-documents.htm?dtl/29495/IndiaIran+Joint+Statement+during+Visit+of+the+President+of+Iran+to+India+February+17+2018

Kazakhstan transport corridor project; on February 3, 2018 India joined to the "Ashgabat Agreement" and became a member of this project.

Meanwhile, the weak link of the Chabahar project that could limit the potential for its transformation into the main transport hub for trade between India and Central Asia is the lack of access to the railway network of Iran and the Central Asian states. The construction of the railway, along with the development of port infrastructure and the construction of industrial enterprises would become one of the key tasks of Iran-India cooperation in the long term. In the initial stages, trade would be by road, but it would be more expensive than rail transportation, and would make trade costlier.

Thus Indian Prime Minister Narendra Modi, during negotiations with the Iranian president, stated that Delhi "fully supports the construction of the Chabahar-Zahedan railway line, so that the Chabahar potential as a transport gate would be fully used".[32] In particular, an initial agreement was signed between the Islamic Republic of Iran and India, in which the Indian side agreed to invest $2 billion in the development of the ports and railways of Iran. One of the points of the agreement was the plans to invest $800 million in the construction of the Chabahar-Zahedan railway.[33]

In terms of land and maritime routes that can connect Indian port facilities to Shahid Beheshti (Chabahar) with the transport system of Central Asian countries, there are three connecting points.

The first is a land corridor through Turkmenistan, through which most of the cargo is handled via the "Central Asia-Iranian ports of the Persian Gulf" and "Central Asia-Iran-Turkey" lines. Within this corridor, goods are transported both by road and rail.

The docking of the railway systems of Central Asia and Iran in the Turkmen corridor is currently carried out through two border

---

32 India, Iran sign pact during Rouhani visit on leasing port by Manoj Kumar. February 17, 2018. https://www.reuters.com/article/us-india-iran/india-iran-sign-pact-during-rouhani-visit-on-leasing-port-idUSKCN1G10GS

33 Indians to invest $2 billion in Iran's port, railways. February 17, 2018. https://en.mehrnews.com/tag/Abbas+Akhoundi

crossings - Serakh and Akyaila/Inche Burun. The Tejen-Serakhs-Mashhad railway, commissioned in 1996, is being put into operation via Serakhs, which enables connection of the railway systems of Iran and all five Central Asian countries. The volume of transit traffic along this railway route is growing at a rapid pace. During the period from March 21 to November 21, 2017, 770 thousand tons of cargos passed through Serakhs (province of Khorasan Resavi), which is 80 per cent more in comparison to the same period in 2016. From Central Asia, primarily from Turkmenistan, Uzbekistan and Tajikistan, sulfur, fertilizers, cotton, aluminum ingots and mazut were exported through Serakhs.[34] The importance of the railroad through Serakhs is clear when compared with the total volume of cargo transportation through Iran. For the first 9 months of the Iranian calendar year (from March 21, 2017 to March 21, 2018), the total volume of cargoes that transited through Iran amounted to 1.15 million tons (an increase of 61 per cent), and by the end of the year is likely to be 1.6 million tons.[35]

The Kazakhstan-Turkmenistan-Iran railway line passes through the second Akayla/Ince Burun crossing, which was put into operation in December 2014. Its design capacity is 10 million tons of cargo per year. Operators of the project expect to attract cargoes through the "International North-South Transportation Corridor" from Russia, the Middle East, Southeast Asia, and in the near future from India. A good deal gained from the trade with China. China regularly sends freight trains from its several industrial centres since December 2016 to January 2018. Now the route "China-Kazakhstan-Turkmenistan-Iran" is being tested, the length of which is 10400 km. The test results showed that the time of delivery of goods from the east coast of China to Tehran is on average 14-16 days.

---

34 Транзит железнодорожных грузов через иранский город Серахс вырос на 80 per cent.19 декабря 2017. http://www.iran.ru/news/economics/107916/ Tranzit_zheleznodorozhnyh_gruzov_cherez_iranskiy_gorod_Serahs_vyros_na_80

35 Iran's railroad transit up by 61 per cent. DECEMBER 18, 2017. http://www. themeditelegraph.com/en/transport/road-rail-air-transport/2017/12/18/iran-railroad-transit-vqdljbukKjJrJc8SZ6qbJK/index.html

Iran's Caspian ports - Amirabad, Enseli, Noushehr, Neka, Fereydoon, Kenar, and Sari could be **the second** possible connecting point between the port capacities of India in Chabahar and the transport system of Central Asia, through which the freight could be carried out with the ports of Aktau and Kuryk (Kazakhstan), as well as Turkmenbashi (Turkmenistan).

Iranian authorities have paid much attention to the development of the port of Amirabad in the province of Masandaran. Since 2013, $237 million has been invested in the expansion of the port infrastructure that has increased its handling capacity from 4 to 7.5 million tons per year. This makes Amirabad the largest port on the Caspian Sea and the third largest port in Iran. In 2017 President Hassan Rouhani launched the second phase of the port development project, which envisages the construction of 6 berths capable of handling another 4 million tons of cargo per year. Moreover, the second phase includes additional storage facilities for grain and oil that are to be built. The plan for modernisation of the port of Amirabad envisages to increase its overall capacity to handle cargo to 18 million tons per year by 2030, including an increase in grain storage capacity from 170,000 to 500,000 tons, and oil storage from 16,000 to 70,000 cubic meters. The Iranian authorities consider that one of the key goals of all these investments in Amirabad is to increase the volume of transit of goods from the CIS countries and Central Asia. The advantage of the port is its access to the railway line Amirabad-Garmsar, which connects to the Iranian national railway network and the Kazakhstan-Turkmenistan-Iran railway through Ince Burun.[36]

Iran's total investment in the development of its ports for the 11 months during 2017 and 2018 amounted to $205 million (40 projects), which enabled it to increase their turnover by 7 per cent to 142 million tons.[37] In the next 4 years, Iran plans to increase the

---

36 Iran's Amirabad Port Investments Top $230 Million Since 2013. December 16, 2017. https://financialtribune.com/articles/economy-business-and-markets/77954/irans-amirabad-port-investments-top-230-million-since

37 Port development projects worth $205m implemented in a year. March 12, 2018. http://www.tehrantimes.com/news/421999/Port-development-projects-

aggregate capacity of its ports is 210 to 250 million tons. It may be noted that Shahid Rajai (Persian Gulf) and Jask (Oman Gulf) port modernisation projects, as well as the construction of oil terminals within the above mentioned ports can be used by Central Asian countries, such as Kazakhstan and Turkmenistan, for oil supplies to India and other Asian markets under the "oil swap" scheme.[38]

The third promising connectivity between Chabahar and Central Asia could be Afghanistan, which together with Uzbekistan and Iran is making efforts to create a north-Afghan railway corridor. During the visit of Afghan President Ashraf Ghani to Uzbekistan in December 2017, an agreement was reached on cooperation in the construction of the 760-km-long Mazar-e-Sharif-Shibirgan-Maymana-Herat railway. According to the Deputy Prime Minister of Uzbekistan Jamshid Kuchkarov, the project evaluation had already been completed and negotiations were underway to finance it with the Central Bank and the Asian Infrastructure & Investment Bank.[39] It needs no emphasise that both countries have rich experience in effective cooperation in the railway sector. In 2010 Uzbekistan built the Hayraton-Mazar-e-Sharif railway, with a throughput capacity of 9 million tons of cargo per year with the financial participation of the Asian Development Bank ($165 million).

Iran is also cooperating with Afghanistan for the construction of the Haf-Herat railway that will connect Herat, the largest economic centre of northwestern Afghanistan, with the Iranian railway and port infrastructure. The integration of Iranian and Uzbek projects will create a unified railway network consisting of Iran, Afghanistan, Uzbekistan, Tajikistan, Kyrgyzstan, southern and eastern regions of Kazakhstan and the south-western provinces of China in the long term.

---

worth-205m-implemented-in-a-year

38 Каспийскийрезерв. Maritime news of Russia. http://www.morvesti.ru/analitics/detail.php?ID=63835

39 Узбекистан и Афганистан обсудили строительство железной дороги Мазари-Шариф — Герат. http://podrobno.uz/cat/politic/uzbekistan-i-afganistan-obsudili-stroitelstvo-zheleznoy-dorogi-masari-sharif-gerat/

This unified network will undoubtedly meet the economic and geopolitical interests of India in Central Asia and Afghanistan, especially if the Chabahar-Zahedan and Zahedan-Birdland-Mashhad railways are built with the access to Herat, Mazar-e-Sharif and Uzbekistan. The length of the second route is 730 km, would have a capacity of 12 million tons of cargo per year.[40] Promotion of New Delhi's interests in this area will be facilitated by the fact that India along with Iran and Afghanistan is a party to the tripartite agreement on the creation of an international transport and transit corridor.

The Central Asian states will also be able to derive great economic benefits from the new Afghan route. Southern regions of Uzbekistan, especially, Termez, could become a major transit and export hub; the opening of the Termez Cargo export centre on September 30, 2017 has the products of the Uzbek automobile and textile industry, agricultural equipment, household appliances, furniture, building materials, etc. for trade.[41]

Moreover, Tajikistan and Kyrgyzstan would also be able to draw dividends from the access to the Afghan and Iranian railway systems through Uzbekistan, thereby diversifying their export-import route that increases their opportunity for developing industry and agriculture, attracting foreign investment, including from India. The incentive for developing connectivity between India and Central Asian countries could also involve joint participation in the development of mineral deposits in Afghanistan, located near the north-Afghan railway corridor.

The vulnerability of the North-Afghan corridor is the unstable situation in Afghanistan. Therefore the regional countries are making concerted efforts to facilitate a peace process in that country, wherein it is worth noting the efforts of Uzbekistan. Tashkent organised an international conference on Afghanistan on March 26-27, 2018 in

---

40 Zahedan-Birjand-Mashhad railway.PROJECT PROFILE – SUMMARY SHEET. https://www.investiniran.ir/OIETA_content/fa/pprojects/Zahedan.pdf

41 Узбекистан намерен довести товарооборот с Афганистаном до 1 миллиарда долларов. http://podrobno.uz/cat/economic/uzbekistan-nameren-dovesti-tovarooborot-s-afganistanom-do-1-milliarda-dollarov-/

Tashkent, in which all key actors including India took part to discuss the Afghan political and economic process.

Conclusion

The issue of synchronised development of transport projects and the diversification of the commodity structure of trade between Central Asia and India will become increasingly important as the course for mutually beneficial cooperation strengthens. As the world experience and features of economic globalisation show, strong ties between the leading world economies are based mostly on these two components. Building relations on free trade rules, both through the WTO and the Free Trade Area (FTA) can be a major supportive factor in the development of Indian-Central Asian economic ties. This process is already on -going between India and some of the Central Asian countries.

In June 2017, Kazakhstan and Kyrgyzstan, as members of the Eurasian Economic Union (EEA), signed a statement on the beginning of negotiations with India on the Free Trade Agreement (FTA), which could start in 2018. According to the forecasts of the Eurasian Economic Commission, the establishment of the FTA of the EEA with India will increase bilateral trade by 30-40 per cent,[42] which the creation of FTA between the EEA and Vietnam in October 2016 illustrates, wherein Kazakhstan was a major beneficiary. By successfully using the free trade, Kazakhstan doubled its exports to the Vietnamese market to US \$166 million for the period January–June 2017.[43]

Successful implementation of projects in the field of diversifying the commodity structure of export-import transactions and strengthening foundations of free trade will undoubtedly have a positive impact on the interest of India and the Central Asian

---

42 Алексей Никоноров, Зачем Казахстану свободная торговля с Индией?. 09 июня 2017. https://365info.kz/2017/06/sachem-kasahstanu-svobodnaya-torgovlya-s-indiej/

43 Алексей Никоноров, Казахстан больше всех в ЕАЭС выиграл от сотрудничества с Вьетнамом. 28 сентября 2017, https://365info.kz/2017/09/kasahstan-bolshe-vseh-v-eaes-vyigral-ot-sotrudnichestva-s-vetnamom/

countries in the further development of transport communications through Iran and Afghanistan, as well as on increasing the capacity of their national railways, highways and ports, removing obstacles on the transit of goods. In other words, one breakthrough will serve as a catalyst for a new series of other breakthroughs.

At the same time, in terms of development of trade and transport links between India and Central Asian countries there will still be risks that deserve particular attention – the ongoing Afghan conflict and looming prospects for the resumption of the sanctions on Iran by the West. Therefore, an assessment of political risks will be of particular importance, which may become another area of close bilateral cooperation between the Central Asian states and India.

Prospects For Cooperation on Regional Connectivity, Trade and Transit between India And Uzbekistan – An Indian View

Nirmala Joshi

The world community accorded equal importance of connectivity issues as the present day globalised world order was taking shape. This emphasis on connectivity was in congruence with Indian priorities as well. In her address at the Raisina Dialogue in March 2016, External Affairs Minister Smt. Sushma Swaraj highlighted the significance of connectivity, as India was keen to connect with the Eurasian region especially with the Central Asian Republics (CARs), its strategic/extended neighbourhood. In her words "... Connectivity today is central to the globalisation process. It is of course particularly important for Asia's growth and development ... whether it is domestic, external or regional connectivity will determine how we meet our promise of growth, employment and prosperity".[1] Speaking in a similar vein the then Foreign Secretary Shri S. Jaishankar noted "... Like globalisation connectivity has always existed in human history. What has changed is that we think of it much sharper structured terms".[2]

Today the significance of connectivity is apparent in the vast and

---

1 "Speech by External Affairs Minister at the Inauguration of Raisina Dialogue in New Delhi (March 01, 2016)." Ministry of External Affairs, Government of India. March 01, 2016. Accessed September 05, 2018. https://mea.gov.in/Speeches-Statements.htm?dtl/26432.

2 "Speech by Foreign Secretary at Raisina Dialogue in New Delhi (March 2, 2015)." Ministry of External Affairs, Government of India. March 02, 2016. Accessed September 05, 2018. https://mea.gov.in/Speeches-Statements.htm?dtl/26433.

open Eurasian landmass where major powers have already initiated their connectivity projects criss-crossing the region. Several factors can be ascribed to the changing regional dynamics; importantly the reinvention of British geographer Halford Mackinder's theory of geopolitics. According to his theory the 'Heartlands of Eurasia' and the 'Pivot of History' are critical and will determine the destinies of nations not only of region, but of the world as well. The Pivot of History is Central Asia because of its centrality in Eurasia. There is a view among analysts and observers that Uzbekistan is probably the pivot. Besides the abundance of natural resources and vital minerals in Eurasia, and the landlocked status of most of the nations has stimulated various connectivity projects to secure and possibly control the vital resources. In a way the major connectivity projects are aimed at initially establishing the presence of the main actors and gradually building strategic leverages. In a way this lends credence to Mackinder's theory of geopolitics. Another factor is the CARs geopolitical location flanking two potential powers; the Russian Federation and the Peoples Republic of China, who could challenge the world leadership role of the United States of America. Consequently the CARs have been caught in the vortex of competitive international politics.

As a consequence the transport sector and connectivity projects have become a tool in the hands of the powers who are seeking to reach out to the CARs. However Indian attempts to connect with the CARs are stymied due to the lack of direct connectivity with these nations. In an apt observation Jaishankar, former Foreign Secretary said "by contemporary standards we are significantly an under connected nation. This is a major constraint on both our capabilities and competitiveness".[3]

While various connectivity projects are on the anvil, an equally daunting challenge is posed by the rise of non-traditional threats. It is an ideological challenge to the nation-states of Central Asia and others in the region, and has the potential to destabilise the Eurasian region. The CARs also have to face the challenge posed by extremist forces and terrorism on the one hand and on the other hand to utilise

---

3 Ibid.

the opportunity for economic development by participating in the various on-going projects.

Paradoxically, the trend towards globalisation also accompanies by strengthening regional tendencies. The Central Asian region that includes Afghanistan, as it belongs to the same geopolitical space, is the least integrated. In the region centrifugal tendencies are dominant, than centripetal ones. However, a successful and beneficial outcome of the various projects for the CARs will be evident, if there is vibrant regional cooperation among the nations. Although such cooperation is still a long way off. There is now greater awareness that if they have to progress and become players in their own right, then regional cooperation is essential. It is necessary to harmonise rules and regulations, tariffs, border crossing and control etc. for an effective cooperation. In this regard President Shavkat Mirziyoyev has undertaken active diplomatic initiatives to promote regional cooperation. His efforts are commendable.

In view of Eurasia, it is witnessing fundamental shifts; from cooperation to conflict and presently trade route from the partnership primarily Russia and China who have established their presence. The question is can India overcome its lack of direct connectivity and reach out to the CARs? India has to depend on the goodwill of and friendly ties with third countries to reach out to the CARs. In this regard Iran has shown the way forward. What are India's options? This paper will explore India's options and assess the prospects.

Options for India

The best option would have been to follow the ancient trade route from the Indian subcontinent to Afghanistan. In the past India had flourishing ties with the region which added to its well-being and prosperity. Afghanistan lay on the cross roads of major trade and transport routes. One branch of the ancient trade route went northwards towards Central Asia. In today's context, it would imply crossing Pakistan-Afghanistan and reaching Uzbekistan. However, in view of Pakistan's persistent obduracy in refusing to allow India passage through its territory led to search for a viable alternative. India's reach coincided with Iran's goal to rejuvenate its economy with a focus on infrastructure development. In the process Iran has emerged as the gateway to connect with Central Asia via Afghanistan and Turkmenistan. Iran was keen to develop its second port Chabahar on the Makran coast in the Gulf of Hormuz as Bandar Abbas was getting congested. The best option for India to connect with Uzbekistan is via the Chabahar and Afghan highway – the Garland Highway. From the Indian perspective, linking with Uzbekistan is beneficial as it is centrally located. It shares borders with all the four Republics; therefore, access to them can be facilitated. Moreover,according to a report by the Asian Development Bank (ADB), Uzbekistan's infrastructure is fairly well developed. The railway network in Uzbekistan covers 4230 km. In 2014, in celebrations of its twentieth anniversary, Uzbekistan Railways noted that all regions in the country are connected with railway lines.

The Chabahar Option

On the road map of connectivity, the visit of Prime Minister Narendra Modi to Teheran in May 2016 was historic. The high point was the signing of the Trilateral Transport and Trade Agreement between Afghanistan, India and Iran[4]. The Agreement opened up prospect of overland connectivity for India with Afghanistan, the CARs and beyond. The Trilateral Agreement is considered as a milestone in Indian foreign policy initiatives. As observed by Prime Minister Modi "it could alter the history of the region[5]." While President Hassan Rouhani spoke about the Chabahar port as a "defining partnership which has the potential of connecting the entire region[6]."

The Chabahar opens directly into the Indian Ocean and does

---

4 "India, Iran and Afghanistan Sign Chabahar Port Agreement." Https://www. hindustantimes.com/. May 23, 2016. Accessed September 01, 2018. https:// www.hindustantimes.com/india/india-iran-afghanistan-sign-chabahar-port-agreement/story-2EytbKSeo6seCIpR8WSuAO.html

5 Ibid

6 "Iran Can Be Reliable Partner for India's Energy Needs: Hassan Rouhani." The Economic Times. April 17, 2016. Accessed September 01, 2018. https://economictimes.indiatimes.com/news/economy/foreign-trade/ iran-can-be-reliable-partner-for-indias-energy-needs-hassan-rouhani/ articleshow/51866679.cms.

not have to cross the 'chicken neck' of the Gulf of Hormuz. It is a deep water port and has the capacity to accommodate large ships and tankers. Chabahar is located a mere 1000 km. from Kandla and Mundra on the Gujarat Coast. Its other advantage is that Indian ships can bypass Dubai, thereby avoiding transit tax. From Chabahar a road link of about 600 km. connects the port with Sahidan on the Iran-Afghan border. A road link from Saranj on the Afghan-Iran border connects Sahidan on the one side with Delaram (217 km.) on the Garland Highway. From Delaram the goods are transported to Mazar-i-Sharif by trucks. The 'Friendship Bridge' on the Amu Darya links Mazar-i-Sharif with Hairatan on the Uzbekistan – Afghanistan Border.

Chabahar has two terminals – Shahid Kalantri and Shahid Beheshti. The first terminal is handling about 2.1 million tons of cargo per year and with the operationalisation of the Shahid Beheshti terminal the capacity is expected to increase to about 10 million tons.[7] As part of the Trilateral Agreement, India has signed a MoU on the construction of a railway which is 500 km. It will connect Chabahar with Sahidan by a rail network. After the operationalisation of the Indian berth at the Shahid Beheshti port, India shipped the first consignment of 1.1 million tons of wheat to Afghanistan. The Ministry of External Affairs added "The shipment of wheat is a landmark development as it will pave the way for the operationalisation of the Chabahar as an alternative, reliable and robust connectivity to Afghanistan".[8] The first phase of work on Chabahar was completed by November 2017. The completion phase was marked by a ceremonial inauguration. On this occasion President Rouhani said "… the port will enhance trade in the region with the final aim to connect not just Afghanistan via rail, but also to

---

7   Ambassador P. Stobdan, "To make Chabahar "Game Changer" Central Asian States need to be roped in". 12 December 2017, . Accessed September 01, 2018   http://idsa.in/documents/to-make-Chabaha-a-game-changer-central-asian-states_pstobdan_12 1217.

8   Bhattacherjee, Kallol. "India Ships Wheat to Afghanistan via Chabahar.» The Hindu. October 29, 2017. Accessed September 02, 2018. https://www. thehindu.com/news/national/india-ships-wheat-to-afghanistan-via-chabahar/article19945498.ece. .

the 7,200 km International North South Transport Corridor (INSTC) to Russia".[9] In June 2018, during their meeting on the side lines of the Shanghai Cooperation Organisation (SCO), Prime Minister Modi and President Mirziyoyev expressed the hope to supplement their connectivity through the Chabahar with the establishment of industrial parks and investment zone in Uzbekistan[10].

In a related development, Uzbek State railway company, Ozbekistan Temir Yollari and the Afghan railways have agreed to extend a railway line from Mazar-i-Sharif to Herat for faster connectivity. An agreement to this effect was signed between President Mirziyoyev and Afghan President Ashraf Ghani in Tashkent in December 2017.[11] According to Uzbek expert Zilola Karimova "The construction of the Mazar-i-Sharif-Herat railway and ensuring its effective functioning will contribute to the successful integration of the countries of Central Asia and Afghanistan into international transport and trade systems in several ways".[12] In the perception of Dipanjan Roy Choudhury, an Indian commentator, "it is a win-win situation for both the countries. While Uzbekistan would assist India in its endeavour for smooth connectivity to the region. India could be Uzbekistan's gateway to the seas".[13] However, in view of the

---

9 The Hindu (New Delhi), 29 November 2017.

10 Aneja, Atul. "India, Uzbekistan to Route Their Trade Though Chabahar." The Hindu. June 10, 2018. Accessed September 05, 2018. https://www.thehindu.com/news/international/india-uzbekistan-to-route-their-trade-though-chabahar/article24127666.ece

11 Mamatkulov, Mukhammadsharif. "Uzbekistan Seeks Sea Access with Afghan Railway Deal." Reuters. December 05, 2017. Accessed September 02, 2018. https://in.reuters.com/article/uzbekistan-afghanistan-railway/uzbekistan-seeks-sea-access-with-afghan-railway-deal-idINKBN1DZ29H.

12 Karimova, Zilola. "Connecting Asia: Uzbekistan Looks to Capitalise on Central Asia's Transport Potential." The Diplomat. April 12, 2018. Accessed September 03, 2018. https://thediplomat.com/2018/04/connecting-asia-uzbekistan-looks-to-capitalise-on-central-asias-transport-potential/.

13 "Uzbekistan Seeks to Be India's All-weather Ally in Central Asia.» The Economic Times. March 26, 2018. Accessed September 05, 2018. https://economictimes.indiatimes.com/news/politics-and-nation/uzbekistan-seeks-to-be-indias-all-weather-ally-in-central-asia/articleshow/63472248.cms.

impending sanctions on Iran by the US, it is hoped that expansion plans for the Chabahar will not come under sanctions.

Uzbekistan-Turkmenistan-Iran-Oman Transport Corridor

Apart from the Chabahar option to reach the CARs, the Ashgabat Agreement of 2011 finalised a corridor with a destination in the southern direction. It is the Uzbekistan-Turkmenistan-Iran-Oman transport corridor (often referred to as the Persian Gulf Corridor). The membership of the Ashgabat Agreement as expanded to include Kazakhstan and Pakistan (2016). India's quest to be associated with the Agreement was fulfilled in February 2018[14]. To an extent this corridor resembles the fabled silk route of the fifth century, when caravans passed through Uzbekistan then to Turkmenistan and Iran.

After the assumption of the Presidency by President Mirziyoyev in 2016, the need to energise this corridor gained a new urgency. An independent expert on International Relations Chinara Esengul based in Bishkek observed that President Mirziyoyev did not want isolation for Uzbekistan[15]. In his address to the Oiliy Majlis (Parliament) on 23 December 2017, he paid special attention to the task of "forming reliable transport including transit corridors for the delivery of Uzbekistan's foreign trade goods to the largest markets of the world and the region".[16] In this context the President realised that the country needs more open borders. The President launched hectic diplomatic parleys in search of peaceful borders and stability. In 2017 the President held 17 bilateral and multilateral meetings with

---

14 "India Joins Ashgabat Agreement - Times of India." The Times of India. February 01, 2018. Accessed September 04, 2018. https://timesofindia. indiatimes.com/india/india-joins-ashgabat-agreement/articleshow/62745556. cms

15 Baumgartner, Pete. "Tug-Of-War: Uzbekistan, Kyrgyzstan Look To Finally Settle Decades-Old Border Dispute." RadioFreeEurope/RadioLiberty. December 14, 2017. Accessed September 02, 2018. https://www.rferl.org/a/ uzbekistan-kyrgyzstan-resolving-decades-old-border-dispute/28918059.html

16 Karimova, Zilola. "Connecting Asia: Uzbekistan Looks to Capitalise on Central Asia's Transport Potential." The Diplomat. April 12, 2018. Accessed September 03, 2018. https://thediplomat.com/2018/04/connecting-asia-uzbekistan-looks-to-capitalise-on-central-asias-transport-potential/

Central Asian leaders. The borders with Kyrgyzstan and Tajikistan were in the Fergana Valley which were fractions and dotted with enclaves. These borders are hotly contested, erupting into local violence; a outbreak of violence on the border would result in its prolonged closure and cause tense security conditions. Closure of borders would adversely affect the movement of trucks and would take months of negotiations to reopen them. This also hampered the growth of inter and intra-regional trade and cooperation on issues of cardinal importance to the CARs.

With focus on connectivity Uzbekistan adopted a comprehensive five year programme to improve its transport infrastructure and diversify foreign trade routes in December 2017. An important section of the Persian Gulf transport and communication corridor was launched during President Mirziyoyev's visit to Turkmenistan in March 2017[17]. The Turkmenabad-Farab railway and road bridges across the Amu Darya were also opened, more than doubling the volume of cargo transportation[18]. In addition Uzbekistan plans to extend rail link between Mazar-e-Sharif to Herat. This extension would facilitate the movement of goods and make the corridor efficient. According to Zilila Karimova "The construction of the Mazar-i-Sharif-Herat railway and ensuring its effective functioning will contribute to the successful integration of the countries of Central Asia and Afghanistan into international transport and trade systems in several ways".[19] The issue of regional connectivity was highlighted by President Mirziyoyev in an address to the United Nations General Assembly (UNGA) in September 2017. As the President noted "Central Asia, being in the Heart of Eurasia stands as a bridge connecting Europe and the Middle East, South and East Asia. The region is rich in natural resources. There is a unique cultural and civilisation potential, which has had a decisive influence on the development of many countries and entire regions".[20]

---

17 Ibid

18 Ibid

19 Ibid.

20 Tashkent to Hold a High level Conference on Afghanistan, Press Service of the Ministry of Foreign Affairs of the Republic of Uzbekistan. Accessed

Besides attempting to settle vexatious borders with its neighbours, Uzbekistan has also undertaken, as mentioned, to improve its provincial and district connectivity.

The International North South Transport Corridor

Though a circuitous link for Uzbekistan, the INSTC is an alternate route to reach Uzbekistan. The INSTC connects St. Petersburg with Mumbai and is a multimodal transport corridor; sea, rail and surface transport. Bandar Abbas strategically located on the Persian Gulf is the transit point for the onward journey to Russia. There are two options to reach St. Petersburg either via Azerbaijan or via Turkmenistan and Kazakhstan. Through this route, Indian exports could potentially get competitive advantage due to lower cost and less delivery time.

Though the INSTC is operational, it is not functioning at the desired capacity. Recently,Russia has shown renewed keenness to re-energise the INSTC. One of the highlights of Prime Minister Modi's visit to St. Petersburg in June 2017 was an agreement to revitalise the INSTC[21]. Mention must be made of the rail connectivity between Kazakhstan, Turkmenistan and Iran that has considerably eased the flow of freight. Since the Persian Gulf Corridor is operational, and Turkmenistan has also initiated plans to emerge as a trade and transit hub, it may not be cumbersome for Uzbekistan to connect with the Indian Ocean. President Rouhani mentioned that there are plans to connect INSTC with Chabahar.

Besides, India has regular flights to Tashkent and other capitals. Uzbekistan has declared the city of Navoi in the Northwest as an international airport and has set up special free economic zone in the city. According to reports flights from Mumbai once a week take off for Navoi, carrying cargo mostly from South Korea.

Prospects for India Uzbekistan Cooperation

India and Uzbekistan have had abiding historical ties and cultural

---

September 03, 2018. From https://www.uzbekconsulny.org/consulate/index.php/en/en-news-events.

21 http://pib.nic.in/newsite/PrintRelease.aspx?relid=163331

contacts since centuries. After the establishment of diplomatic ties in the post 1991 era, India's relations with Uzbekistan began to gain an upward trajectory. Uzbekistan along with the other four Republics has perceived India as a friendly country, a balance in the on-going international politics in Eurasia. India and Uzbekistan share the view that economic growth and development in the Central Asia will be the harbinger for stability and security in the long term. As a consequence connectivity issue with the landlocked region is critical. From Uzbekistan's perspective an amicable atmosphere in the region is essential for it to complete its socio-economic and political transformation. "A peaceful Afghanistan is able to ensure the shortest possible access for the nations of Central Asia to harbours of the Indian Ocean and Persian Gulf ...."[22]

A major landmark in this regard was the visit of President Islam Karimov to India in May 2011 when the two countries signed a Strategic Partnership Agreement (SPA). The thrust of the Agreement was on economic development and connectivity. Another landmark development was the enunciation of Connect Central Asia Policy (CCAP) by India in 2012. The policy aimed at enhancing India's strategic space and engagement with the CARs. It raised the earlier conceptual framework of extended neighbourhood to connecting with CARs. The policy operates at two levels; official as well as at the Track II level. The CCAP was unveiled by Minister of State for External Affairs Shri E. Ahmed. At the first India-Central Asia Dialogue in Bishkek in 2012 Shri Ahmed said "India is now looking intently at the region through the framework of Connect Central Asia Policy which is based on proactive political, economic and people to people engagement with the Central Asian countries both individually and collectively". Elucidating further he said "We must factor in the regional situation and especially the challenge of re-building Afghanistan into a hub of trade and energy connecting Central with South Asia".[23] The CARs welcomed the new policy as

22 Press Service of the Ministry of Foreign Affairs of the Republic of Uzbekistan, February 2018.

23 "Keynote Address by MOS Shri E. Ahamed at First India-Central Asia Dialogue." Ministry of External Affairs, Government of India. June 12, 2012. Accessed September 03, 2018. https://www.mea.gov.in/Speeches-Statements.

there was a wide area of shared interests on issues of regional security and stability. The significance of CCAP was not at the bilateral level, but importantly it was a first regional initiative launched by India.

India's membership of the SCOhas further widened the prospects of increasing engagement with the CARs including Uzbekistan especially on issues of regional connectivity. In his acceptance speech on India's membership of the SCO, the Prime Minister stressed the issue of connectivity. He said "connectivity with the SCO countries is India's priority and we strongly support it .... Our involvement with the INSTC and Chabahar Agreement and our decision to join the Ashkhabad agreement will bring India closer to the region".[24] Today India's CCAP has moved to a higher level "Think West".

With twenty five years down the line, Uzbekistan's increasing focus is on connectivity in the southern direction, an opening on the Indian Ocean the hub of trade and investment. This issue has acquired a new urgency as Uzbekistan's young population is rising (in the age group of 25 to 50), it is between 40-42 per cent, and with this rise is also the growing expectation of the people. This critical mass has access to internet; some are travelling abroad for higher studies, and have new innovative ideas. They are capable of contributing to the nation building process. It would enable this critical mass to be gainfully employed. Such an approach will, at least, keep some youth away from being attracted to extremism.

President Mirziyoyev has accorded therefore the highest priority to economic development. His approach is to make Uzbekistan an investor friendly country. The areas of focus are electric power, chemical and petrochemical production including fertilisers, transport services among other industrial sectors. Uzbekistan has created two free industrial and economic zones to attract foreign investment at Navoi and Angren. Importantly Uzbekistan has also

---

htm?dtl/19791/.

24 "English Rendition of Prepared Text of Press Statement by ..." MEA. June 09, 2017. Accessed September 5, 2018. http://www.mea.gov.in/Speeches-Statements.htm?dtl/28518/English_rendition_of_Prepared_text_of_Press_Statement_by_Prime_Minister_at_SCO_Summit_in_Astana_June_09_2017.

undertaken economic reforms to ease the flow of investments. These areas are starting business dealing with construction permits, protecting small investors, paying taxes etc.[25]

With the growing congruence of interests, the prospects for cooperation between India and Uzbekistan have brightened considerably. With Uzbekistan's priority on economic development the opportunity for India to engage with Uzbekistan has opened up. For instance the industrial, agricultural, infrastructure development is areas where cooperation between the two countries will be productive. At the regional level, India's membership of the SCO has given it a presence in the Central Asian region. Probably, the connectivity issue can gain momentum as it is part of the SCO agenda.

Intertwined with regional connectivity is the question of cooperation among the CARs. In this regard President Mirziyoyev has taken a new approach and accorded a priority to regional cooperation and economic integration. On his initiative, an important conference of the countries was held at Astana in March 2018. President Nursultan Nasarbaev pointed out "in order to solve the problems of Central Asia, we do not need any third persons. We ourselves can solve all questions and that is why we are meeting".[26] Whereas President Mirziyoyev mapped out six regional priorities; (1) increasing intra-regional trade, (2) developing transportation infrastructure that connects the region with world markets, (3) cooperating on security issues ..., (4) completing border demarcation and delimitation, (5) regularising trans-boundary water issues and (6) developing close neighbourly relations.[27]

---

25 "Economies in Central Asia Continue Reform Agenda." World Bank. November 01, 2017. Accessed September 05, 2018. http://www.worldbank. org/en/news/press-release/2017/11/01/economies-in-central-asia-continue-reform-agenda. .

26 Goble, Paul. "Central Asia Ready to Move on without Russia." Www.timesca. com. March 22, 2018. Accessed September 05, 2018. https://www.timesca. com/index.php/news/26-opinion-head/19516-central-asia-ready-to-move-on-without-russia.

27 Eurasia Daily Monitor.

As mentioned Central Asia is the least integrated region. There is a greater realisation that regional cooperation is essential; firstly, for economic growth and development as they including Afghanistan are landlocked; and, secondly such cooperation will ensure that the external powers will not be able to treat them as 'objects' in the great game of Eurasia, but as subjects entities in their own right. This strategic thinking on the part of CARs could change the dynamics of the Central Asian region.

Conclusion

India's efforts to connect with Uzbekistan have made considerable progress. A combination of fortuitous developments augured well to connect with Uzbekistan and the Central Asian region. The Trilateral Transport and Trade Agreement between Afghanistan, India and Iran of May 2016 was a path breaking one. The Trilateral Agreement opened up vast opportunities to connect with Afghanistan and Central Asia. Plans for expanding this artery by exploring newer options will ease the flow of transport and trade, and also open up prospects for people to people contacts. It is hoped that the impending sanctions by the U S will not affect Chabahar port or its future expansion plans. Secondly, President Shavkat Mirziyoyev's positive approach to the region and regional security, and economic development will go a long way in removing the cobwebs that were affecting ties with the other countries, and regional cooperation as well. His hectic diplomatic parleys with neighbouring countries and persistent efforts to solve the contentious issues with neighbours are, undeniably, indications that he has accorded the highest priority to the region,regional cooperation and economic integration. Such an approach could shape the future of not only, of the region, but could importantly impact on the evolving Eurasian politics. Thirdly, economic development of Uzbekistan is showing promise of progress. Importantly, the economy has reached a stage of its development where its ability to absorb high and innovative technology has grown. Today there is an increase in population in the younger age group. They are well equipped with new methods and can contribute to the country's socio-economic and political processes. This critical mass could be gainfully employed in the development of the country.

India could contribute in terms of further skill development and capacity building measures. Indian investments in agriculture, industrial development and infrastructure could add to the stability and security of Uzbekistan and the region. This is a goal shared by both India and Uzbekistan. .

In the context of changing regional dynamics, connectivity has assumed a critical importance for the landlocked Uzbekistan. It would like an opening in the southern direction — the hub of trade and investment. Moreover it is necessary to intensify its engagement with market potential countries. This would require an effective and an efficient transport corridor. This is absolutely essential in order to attract investments and for export purposes as well. In turn it will promote regional cooperation. The compatibility of mutual interests especially on transport corridor will enable the two countries to pursue their goals in a sustained manner. The momentum of requisite political will by both the sides should not be lost.

SECTION – IV

Effective Management of Islamic Radicalisation of Youth – Uzbekistan's view

Timur Akhmedov

Youth is the engine of social progress and affects sustainability of countries directly. At the same time, the influence of social, political, economic and other problems among youth makes them vulnerable to radical views and convictions.

Most of the extremist activities and violence are committed by the people under the age of 30[1]. According to experts, there are about three hundred thousand representatives of the younger generation in the ranks of Religious Extremist Organisations (REO) who have not yet reached the age of 18. The average age of the European population prone to radicalism, however is noted among the people of in the age group of 28-35 years[2].

The main reasons for such trend are the lack of maturity, the spread and reach of the Internet, dissemination of REO ideas on the Internet and social networks, absence of sufficient inbuilt media safeguard and media immunity from radical views amongst the youths.

According to the Under-Secretary-General for Political Affairs J.Feltman, there are almost fifty thousand accounts supporting the so-called "Islamic State" on Twitter.

The report of Brookings Institution (Washington) indicates that

---

1 President Shavkat Mirziyoyev addressed the 72nd Session of the United Nations General Assembly, Uzbekistan National news agency – https://mfa.uz/en/press/news/2017/09/12493/.

2 Xenophobia, radicalism and hate crimes in Europe in 2016. - M .:Editus, 2017. – XX c.

there are ninety thousands accounts which in one way or another are connected with the IS in Twitter[3]. Each has an average of a thousand readers, and a significant part of these Internet resources are young men and girls.

The youth, due to its social characteristics and acuity of perception is the most vulnerable to such negative anti-social content and protest movements. Taking the dangers into account, Uzbekistan has codified the process of protecting human rights and freedom, ensuring security, interethnic harmony and tolerance as the essence of the new policy.

According to Prof. F.Starr, the Chairman of the Institute of Central Asia and the Caucasus at the University and S.Cornell, the director of this institution, Uzbekistan has established the foundations for an important and unprecedented new direction and model for the Muslim world. The President of Uzbekistan Sh.Mirziyoyev has taken effective steps in solving the problem of extremism. The national idea of "Enlightened Islam" was launched and the government focused on Uzbekistan's special tradition of "moderate" Hanafi Islam[4].

Some of the aspects of "the Enlightened Islam" are looked at positively by international human rights organisations. The Executive Director of Human Rights Watch K. Roth in the annual report in 2018 noted that a number of positive facets in the ongoing reforms in the religious sphere in Uzbekistan.

Moreover, about seventeen thousand people who have become "target" of religious extremist movements have been excluded from the "special lists" of law-enforcement bodies of the country. As the expert notes, President Sh.Mirziyoyev highly emphasised the need

---

3   J.M. Berger and Jonathon Morgan. "The ISIS Twitter census: defining and describing thepopulation of ISIS supporters on Twitter" // The Brookings Institution.

4   S. Frederick Starr and Svante E. Cornell, "Uzbekistan: A New Model for Reform in the Muslim World", The Central Asia-Caucasus Institute and Silk Road Studies Programme – https://www.silkroadstudies.org/resources/pdf/publications/1805FT-UZ-3.pdf

of returning of these "misled" people to normal life[5].

Tashkent considers the fight against extremism and radicalism as an important point for ensuring global security. The President of Uzbekistan Sh.Mirziyoyev has repeatedly noted that ignorance and intolerance lie at the heart of international terrorism and extremism. The most important task is the formation of consciousness and the upbringing of young people through education[6].

While addressing the 72nd session of the UN General Assembly in September 2017, Sh. Mirziyoyev emphasised that creation of conditions for self-realisation of the youth prevents the spread of the "virus" of the ideology of violence.

In order to develop the multilateral cooperation in the sphere of social support for the younger generation, protection of their rights and interests, it was proposed to develop the UN International Convention on the Rights of Youth and the adoption of a special resolution of the General Assembly on "Education and Religious Tolerance"[7].

As Dr. Meena Singh Roy, of the Institute for Defense Studies and Analyses (IDSA), India points out; greater emphasis is given to promoting tolerance, interfaith dialogue and co-existence. There are 136 ethnic groups residing in Uzbekistan and the government is trying to harmonise the lives of all these groups. There are around 100 cultural centres and education is imparted in seven languages. There are 1902 schools offering education in the Russian language, 373 in Kazakh, 361 in Karakalpak, 1104 in Tajik, 91 in Kyrgyz and 44 in Turkmen language. There are also special lyceums for in-depth study of Korean and Hebrew[8].

---

5   Kenneth Roth, Executive Director Human Rights Watch "World Report 2018: The Pushback Against the Populist Challenge" – https://www.hrw.org/ru/world-report/2018/country-chapters/313738

6   Выступление Президента Узбекистана на 72-й сессии Генассамблеи ООН – https://www.un.org/press/en/2017/ga11947.doc.htm

7   Выступление Президента Узбекистана на 72-й сессии Генассамблеи ООН – https://www.un.org/press/en/2017/ga11947.doc.htm.

8   Meena Singh Roy, "Preventing and Countering Violent Extremism: The

The Centre for Islamic Civilisation and international research centres have been established in Uzbekistan to study the true essence of Islam and the realisation of the idea of "Enlightened Islam".

According to Mohd Yusuf Hozhi bin Usman, the director of Malaysian Institute of Islamic Civilisation, Uzbekistan is a country of great thinkers who made a great contribution to the development of holy Islam.

A fact recognised by the entire Muslim world. In this regard, it is very pertinent to learn from Uzbekistan's experience in combating religious extremism and terrorism by effectively using the power of education and spirituality to protect young people from radicalisation[9].

60 per cent of population of Uzbekistan consists of the youth, which is considered to be a "strategic resource of the state". Accordingly, a special policy has been developed and implemented for young citizens of Uzbekistan.A unique system has been created in all regions, districts and cities of Uzbekistan, wherein the representatives of all branches of power are engaged in the implementation of the youth policy in:

- **The system of legislative power**: the Legislative Chamber of the Oliy Majlis (Parliament) has established the Commission for Youth Affairs;

- **The system of executive power**: the position of deputy hokims (governors) was introduced on issues of social sphere, spiritual enlightenment and youth;

- **The system of law enforcement bodies**: the position of deputy head of administration/ department of internal affairs on youth issues was introduced;

"Uzbek Model" – https://thedispatch.co.in/preventing-and-countering-violent-extremism-the-uzbek-model-2/

9 The official website of the Embassy of the Republic of Uzbekistan in Singapore, Daily news bulletin № 117 – http://singapore.mfa.uz/ru/pressroom/news/digest/5185/

- **The system of judiciary**: councils of youth leaders have been elected in the Supreme Judicial Council and the Supreme Court of the Republic, which deal with protection of the rights and interests of the younger generation;

- **The self-government system of citizens**: there are advisors of aksakal on issues of youth in each mahalla (municipality), who are considered deputy chairmen of makhalla.

The core body in the implementation of youth policy is Uzbekistan Youth Union. More than 10 million youth are the members of this Union. The main goal of the organisation is to provide young people with democratic, political, and further economic reforms, peace and harmony in society and independence. The development of Uzbekistan as one of the world's most advanced states, ensuring of freedom and legitimate rights of the younger generation, effective protection of their interests, raise the level of their spiritual and professional qualities, increasing intellectual and creative abilities[10].

The Chairman of the Central Council of the Union is The State Counselor of the President on Youth Affairs, and a member of the Senate of the Oliy Majlis (national parliament) of the Republic of Uzbekistan. Uzbekistan Youth Union cooperates with other public organisations, and also provides support to youth whose parents have been under the influence of religious extremist movements. In particular, about ten thousand such young people were employed[11], 1.54 billion soums were granted for two hundred young people to start their business.

The main goal of the state youth policy is - "no young man should be left without attention."

This goal is in tune with the UNICEF initiative to develop a "Youth Program" that is dedicated to ensure that by 2030 every youth is employed or has been employed in the system of science

---

10 Charter of Uzbekistan Youth Union – http://yi.uz/page/Charter.

11 Meena Singh Roy, "Preventing and Countering Violent Extremism: The "Uzbek Model" – https://thedispatch.co.in/preventing-and-countering-violent-extremism-the-uzbek-model-2/

or education.

As a result of this initiative, in January-May 2018 the number of registered terrorist crimes by people under the age of 30 decreased to 65.7 per cent in comparison with the same period in 2017.

This context has drawn the attention of many countries of Central Asia and other countries in combating threats of extremism and terrorism. International and regional organisations initiate various reports to share about Uzbekistan's experience in its efforts to prevent radicalisation of youth. Raising awareness and formulating policy recommendations to involve and empower youth to prevent their involvement in violent extremism and radicalisation leading to terrorism, was the focus of an international conference held on June 11-12, 2018, Tashkent and Samarkand.

The event was organised by the Organisation for Security and Cooperation in Europe (OSCE) and the UN.

The Secretary General of the OSCE T.Greminger stressed the importance of developing comprehensive and coordinated measures to prevent violent extremism and to fight against terrorism. The OSCE Secretary General appreciated the initiative taken by of Uzbekistan in this sphere[12].

At the end of the conference, the Samarkand Declaration "On increasing the role of youth in countering violent extremism and radicalisation leading to terrorism" was signed. The participants of the conference agreed on the following.

First, counter-proliferation of the ideology of violent extremism among young people and their radicalisation must include a system of institutional, legal, political, socio-economic and information measures, integrate genuine democratic reforms, guarantees for the protection of human rights, economic liberalisation, ensuring decent education.

Second, active work with young people should be central focus

12 Official website OSCE "Uzbekistan hosts OSCE-supported international conference on role of youth in countering violent extremism and radicalisation that lead to terrorism" – https://www.osce.org/secretariat/384219

of governments, parliaments, and international organisations. At the same time the most important task is to ensure all conditions for the self-realisation among the youth, their enlightenment and education, the formation of tolerant consciousness and behavior.

Third, an effective response to the problems of violent extremism and terrorism should not be based on force. The implementation of preventive mechanism and prevention is a more effective method to neutralise the growing challenges of violent extremism and terrorism.

The emergence of new threats in international terrorism and violent extremism in various parts of the world calls for further intensification of joint efforts to combat this negative phenomenon. No state can by itself resist violent extremism and terrorism. In this age of transnational threats to peace and stability, the need is to take adequate multilateral efforts, and deepen international engagement in the area of countering against radicalisation of youth lead to terrorism.

Uzbekistan has time and again drawn the attention of the international community on the key problems faced by the youth. Thus, at the summit of the SCO heads in Qingdao, the 'Appeal to the Youth' was adopted under the initiative of the President of Uzbekistan. The document indicates that young people have become the object of intense attention of destructive forces; they are subjected to massive information, ideological and psychological pressure. In this regard, the leaders of the SCO countries noted that to effectively negate these threats against the youths, and to strengthen immunity to radical ideas, it is necessary to complement the efforts of the member-states with that of public organisation, media, religious communities, educational and scientific institutions of the SCO member states.

This initiative has also been supported by international organisations, in particular, the UN. J.Wikramanayake, the Special Envoy of the UN Secretary General on Youth stated that the UN supports the initiatives of the President Sh.Mirziyoyev at the 72nd session of the UN General Assembly, and at the meeting of the Council of Heads of

State of the SCO in Qingdao. He also mentioned that Uzbekistan had established a strong legal framework aimed at ensuring the interests of the youths. This would form the foundation for the Uzbek youth to get a decent place in society and in the world.

Many experts concur that the "Uzbek model" to counter the threats of extremism, radicalisation, and terrorism amongst the youths is based on an effort to combat the root causes, rather than their consequences. Hence, there is a significant increase in the interest amongst these experts to study this model.

The experience of Uzbekistan to combat and prevent violent extremism and terrorism is to bring the humanistic essence of Islam, the true values of Islamic culture to the youth, as well as the prestige of education in the society and encourage young people to strive for self-improvement, which is the key to achieving sustainable and stable development.

The eradication of religious extremism ideology must be implemented on the basis of a stronger, more reasoned and scientifically based ideology based on a true interpretation of the sacred Islamic writings and knowledge. The initiatives of Sh.Mirziyoyev at the 72nd session of the UN General Assembly on the development of the UN International Convention on the Rights of Youth and the adoption of a special resolution of the General Assembly "Education and Religious Tolerance" are of great importance for the continuation of this work at a qualitative level. The main task of the state and society in this regard is to fight for the minds of people, especially the youths. The youth today in the world is touching two billion populations, the largest generation in history.

Effective Management of Islamic Radicalisation of Youth

Dr Adil Rasheed

The origins, scope and impact of global jihadism extend beyond conventional security and military paradigms and diverge into religious, political, sociological and even historical vectors.

A purely militaristic and security-centric response to the threat often proves inadequate and in some cases counter-productive. Thus, even after decades of militarily degrading and destroying the human and material assets of various jihadist organisations, the swamp of Islamist terrorism continues to spew more radical and virulent forms of violence on the global scene, ever more adept in new modes of warfare and in spreading its influence worldwide.

As extremism and terrorism thrive in an atmosphere of violence and confusion, governments around the world are now seriously pursuing a smarter and more comprehensive approach, by opening ideological, sociological and psychological frontiers in the campaign against violent extremism and terrorism.

Most governments have rightly realised the phenomenon of radicalisation being at the root of jihadist terrorism and have launched various anti-radicalisation, counter-radicalisation and de-radicalisation campaigns around the world. The attempt is to drain the swamp of extremist ideology from which various terrorist organisations rear their heads.

This paper will try to study factors that are influential in the radicalisation of youth, as per the study of various social scientists, activists and strategic experts.

It would then delve into the measures taken by India to counter jihadist radicalisation within the country and then address ways and means for preventing the youth bulge from becoming a demographic bomb in order to yield demographic dividend.

Catching them young

Young people are historically known for being restive and for having problems with authority figures. In the struggle to develop their own identities they often clash with existing social and political hierarchies and conventions. The proverbial 'rebels without a cause' purposely make unconventional fashion statements, even develop counter cultures and alternate political and religious ideologies in order to upset the socio-cultural applecart.

The typical young rebel often comes from well-to-do households, having lived a protected childhood with longstanding idealised conceptions of the self and the world. The late exposure to life's travails shocks the sensitive soul, turning it into an impetuous or reclusive social misfit.

The physiological changes taking place in a person transitioning from a child into an adult also create internal psychological turmoil and impulsiveness in action and behavior.

It is in such a sensitive and vulnerable stage of internal confusion and moral indeterminacy that violent and extremist groups deliver their radical message to wean away impressionable minds from society.

Therefore, it is only natural that jihadist organisations rely on this passionate and malleable section of the population to build up their militant cadres.

Intrepid, idealistic and often overconfident, young minds are generally more prone to taking extreme action without thinking through the consequences — the very qualities terrorist organisations require of their members.

In fact, modern jihadist groups are quite adept at preying upon the aforementioned psychological vulnerabilities that many young people face while growing up.

Exploiting the internal struggles of the adolescent and the young, these groups provide the fledgling personality with a false sense of belonging through group solidarity and the notion of a higher calling and power very early in life.

Parenting problems

Many social scientists and activists have pointed out that young individuals coming from ultra-orthodox and conservative households generally have a hard time navigating their way in a society built on liberal values. Some claim this is particularly the case with young men raised in most Muslim households.

Alyas Karmani, the Co-Director of STREET-UK (Strategy to Reach, Empower And Educate Teenagers), posits that Muslim households around the world generally face problems in raising adolescent children.[1] Having inherited a culture that previously married off children early in life, these parents lack requisite skills to manage the transition of children into adulthood.

The young often unemployed adult children continue to stay on within the confines of their overbearing patriarchal households. Thus, fractured "parent-son, mother-daughter" relations are quite the norm in modern Muslim families.

"Directive and prescriptive type of parenting is common across Muslim cultures. There is a lack of individualism in these societies and parents live vicariously through their children," Karmani claims[2]. Many of these families also try to define their children and map out their entire future for them, even choosing their marriage partners, which vexes relations.

As orthodox Muslim families try to insulate their children from the more permissive values of modern society, their children start

---

1   James Fitzgerald, Frontline perspectives on preventing violent extremism: an interview with Alyas Karmani (STREET UK), Critical Studies on Terrorism journal, Vol. 9, 2016, pp. 139-149

2   Alyas Karmani, The Human Face of Radicalisation, FUUSE Forum, June 28, 2016, https://www.youtube.com/watch?v=bWsyCvDrQBQ

questioning double standards their parents display while themselves interacting with the outside world. This leads to tensions between parents and children, as the latter become increasingly estranged from the family. The young even start upstaging their overbearing parents at their own game, proving to be more ardent and punctilious believers. "Bisarrely," says Karmani: "Violent jihad is a form of personal expression (for these youth)".[3]

In order to compensate for their parents, particularly fathers who appear to be falling short of their own avowed principles, many young radicals join ultra-extremist and radical groups, unbeknownst to their own families. In this bid, "they try to overcompensate and idealise surrogate father figures (leaders of extremist groups). They latch on to gangs and jihadist groups, who they see as surrogate families and their powerful male figures become surrogate father figures," Karmani adds.

Youth coming from tightly-knit conservative families even show signs of 'double life'. "From a very young age Muslim kids learn to have a double role. Nice respectability, going to the mosque, even having an arranged marriage to satisfy their parents and subsequent to that a clandestine existence, hidden in dark and ungoverned spaces". Thus, many times people are taken aback on learning that their well-behaved Muslim neighbor or even family member carried out a terrorist attack.

Simplistic radical messaging

Other noted psychologists and sociologists posit that young radicals often suffer more from personality disorders and identity crisis and have very little understanding of even their own religion or the complexities of politics.

Dr Lorne Dawson, co-director of the University of Waterloo's Canadian Network for Research on Terrorism, Security and Society has interviewed many radicalised jihadists and is of the view that sociological factors play a critical role in turning an average person into a terrorist. According to him, the road

---

3   Ibid

to radicalisation starts with an identity crisis.

"Most of them (young jihadist fighters he interviewed in Syria) explained that they came from what they called comfy or privileged backgrounds; they felt their families were well enough off ... Half of them had gone to college or university and 33 percent had a university degree."[4]

Although they might be angered by a sense of persecution of Muslims, few show the ability to understand the complexities of politics and war. "The choice to go (to foreign war theatres) is theirs, but they're vulnerable to some manipulation," says Dr Dawson.

To a mind riddled with confusion and doubt, terrorist groups provide highly emotive and simplistic solutions that give the illusion of certitude and purpose to confused young minds.

"Salafi jihadists offer a really clean, simple answer: If you want to achieve paradise, you must defend your fellow Muslims against persecution, and that means you have a personal obligation to take up violent means to do that," the sociologist professor avers. "I've read this literature. It's very persuasive. It's easy to imagine how an angry 18-year-old could find it very convincing."[5]

Unlike most of their peers, young radicalised minds feel alienated by the culture around them. "There's this constant theme about moral corruption in the West, about feeling morally challenged and tempted and about needing to find the right, clear path if they want to achieve salvation," says Dr Dawson.

'Death wish': The modern malaise

Noted French political scientist and a leading expert on political Islam, Olivier Roy contends that the problem of radicalisation has little to do with the religion of Islam.

According to him: "Many of these (jihadist) converts, I would

---

4 Claire Prime, 'Radicalisation starts with teen identity crisis for some youth', Waterloo Stories, University of Waterloo, May 23, 2017, https://uwaterloo.ca/stories/radicalisation-starts-teen-identity-crisis-some-youth

5 Ibid

say 30 years ago … would have become extreme left radicals. They would have joined the extreme left. In the 1960s in Western Europe we had a tradition of youth radicalisation from the Marxist revolution. Suddenly around the 1990s, the dream of the Marxist revolution disappeared and al-Qaeda and ISIS filled the vacuum. The problem here is not so much a religious issue. It is one of lack of radical alternative".[6]

Over a century ago, another French sociologist Emile Durkheim highlighted the absence of an alternate ideology to Western capitalism that he blamed led young people to develop radical ideas, even suicidal tendencies.

In his seminal work *Le Suicide*[7] written in 1897, Durkheim looked into one of the most inexplicable conundrums of his times that as countries become wealthier and more industrialised, the rate of depression and suicide also increased. Even today, many Nordic countries of Europe with highest indices of 'happiness' have ironically very high rates of mental illness and suicide rate, particularly in the age group between 16 to 24 years[8].

Durkheim found several factors that lay behind the unhappiness of people in modern societies and their reversion to religion and pre-modern ways of living. According to him, the breakdown of social structures and families in a highly competitive environment and rise of individualism creates sense of insecurity in the population, particularly among the young.

The failure to achieve professional success and financial prosperity weighs heavily upon minds, as it is believed capitalism makes it easy for anybody to be economically successful. Durkheim contends that education and intelligence does not always provide the comfort and solace that religion, mythology and strong familial

---

6 Olivier Roy, 'Terrorists don't come from India's Muslims', rediff. Com, December 1, 2017, http://www.rediff.com/news/interview/terrorists-dont-come-from-indias-muslims/20171201.htm

7 Emile Durkheim (1897) *Suicide : a study in sociology.* The Free Press [1951]. .

8 Why Nordic countries might not be as happy as you think, 25 August 2018. BBC News, https://www.bbc.co.uk/news/world-europe-45308016

and tribal structures do. Thus, according to Durkheim, religious groups have always "established strong community ties of thought and action, virtually eliminated individual divergences, and thus achieved a high degree of unity, solidarity, and integration,"[9] than rationality-driven individualistic societies of the modern age, which promotes free enquiry and thereby creating confusion and existential angst.

According to some modern social scientists, young people are moving towards religious ideologies and atavistic social structures as nation-states are weakening in a globalizing world and as part of the post-modern rebellion of the millennial generation against 20th century neo-liberalism.

In fact, many social philosophers have found Al-Qaeda to have greater affinities with post-modern neo-Marxism than with traditional Islam.[10]

Salafi-Jihadism: The Militant Narrative

Sceptical of some of the arguments presented by sociologists, strategic experts of global jihad find youth radicalisation a direct consequence political changes taking place in the Middle East, at least since the end of World War I, with the dissolution of the Ottoman caliphate and the rise of weak nation-states, leading to the ascendance of Saudi Arabia and Iran as two rival sectarian theocracies.

In addition, the birth of ideological movements like the Muslim Brotherhood in Egypt have rallied generations of religiously radicalised Arab youth into overturning the despotic regimes of the region for instituting modern Shariah-based polities.

Thus, political scientists put the onus of extremist radicalisation and terrorism squarely on the rise of modern Islamism by radical ideologues, like Hasan Al Banna, Syed Qutb and Maulana Maududi.

---

9 Robert Alun Jones. *Emile Durkheim: An Introduction to Four Major Works.* Beverly Hills, CA: Sage Publications, Inc., 1986. Pp. 82-114

10 Richard A. Cohen, Is Al-Qaeda Post-Modern?, The Review of Faith and International Affairs, Volume 5, 2007, Issue 1

These religious and political activists of the 20th century coined a new version of Islam which like communism was projected as a political system for the modern world, as opposed to being a religion.

This ideological transformation was further accelerated with the evolution of the extremist Salafi-Wahhabi ideology, which does not subscribe to any of the four classical schools of Sunni Islam (Hanafi, Shafai, Malaki or Hanbali), let alone the Jafari school of jurisprudence of the Shiites.

The Salafi-Jihadist ideologues are said to have constructed an extremist political and militaristic narrative, aimed at replacing Western liberal and capitalist order with the institution of a global Caliphate as the desired end state.

To this end, a methodology of asymmetric warfare has been promulgated, legitimizing terrorism and genocide as legitimate action, that are strictly forbidden by all classical schools of Islamic jurisprudence.

Various Salafi jihadist ideologues such as Syed Qutb, Mohammad Farag, Abdullah Azsam, Abu Musab Al Suri, Osama bin Laden, Abu Musab Al Sawahiri, Abu Bakr Naji and Abu Bakr Baghdadi have over the decades issued self-styled and religiously unfounded 'fatwas' over the last century to legitimise various forms of warfare that are strictly proscribed in Islam.

However, the young and impressionable minds that are untrained in Islamic law find the ideology and violent campaigns of the Salafi-jihadist groups appealing, as they see them as the only affirmative form of resistance against continued Western military ingress into Muslim lands.

To their young and credulous initiates, jihadist groups hand out books such as *The Economic System of Islam*, wherein Taqiuddin Nabhani details the 'inherent structural' problems dogging the debt and speculation based financial system of our times and advocates replacing the fractional reserve system of banking with his 'non-usurious' theoretical construct.

In his infamous book *Milestones* (Ma'alim fi Al-Tariq),[11] Sayyid Qutb speaks of the incompatibility of Islam with the ideals of nationalism, capitalism and socialism and calls for the violent overthrow of most Muslim potentates. Similarly, the *Laws of Islamic Governance* (Al-Ahkam As-Sultaniyyah) by Al-Mawardi enunciates the tenets of Islamist polity and administration for an ideal caliphate, while Abu Bakr Naji's *Management of Savagery[12]* explores ways of employing terrorism in order to whittle down the morale of Western armies in a protracted war of attrition.

All these works are riddled with theological distortions and fallacies, but little work has been done to challenge these narratives at the ideological level. It is even surprising that much of this foundational literature is easily accessible, even in the English language on the Internet.

Online radicalisation

Terrorist organisations are fully alive to the addictive almost obsessive compulsive appeal the millennial generations have with the internet and therefore have invested heavily in reaching out, identifying, inveigling and radicalising vulnerable young minds across the globe through the Internet by means of their seductive messaging.

Notwithstanding their obscurantist and atavistic discourse, jihadist organisations make full use of the Internet for a variety of purposes. For one, they have a strong presence in the so-called 'Dark Web' (part of the World Wide Web not indexed by Web search engines), which provides the perfect 'breeding ground' for sowing the seeds of radicalisation among young and impressionable minds.

---

11 Syed Qutb Shaheen, *Milestones*, Islamic Book Service, 2017

12 Abu Bakr Naji, The Management of Savagery: The Most Critical Stage Through Which The Umma Will Pass, Translation by William McCants, John M. Olin Institute for Strategic Studies at Harvard University, 2006

Most jihadist groups use the Internet for the purposes of[13]:

1. propaganda;

2. scouting prospective radical recruits from the global throng, otherwise difficult to identify and contact in real world;

3. indoctrination and radicalisation;

4. terror financing, mainly through cryptocurrencies;

5. providing instructions for combat training and weapons manufacturing (particularly from objects of everyday use);

6. carrying out cyberattacks (although incidents of hacking have been few and of relatively very limited impact);

7. coordinating terrorist attacks; and

8. marshalling forces during active operations in theatres such as Syria, Iraq and Libya.

Several empirical studies conducted worldwide show that online radicalisation is the most important means for starting the radicalisation process of individuals in order to involve them into the process of violent extremism.

With the emergence of internet and the spawning of myriad social media platforms, extremist content is spreading far beyond traditional means of communication. As a medium of communication it allows anonymity of identity and can improve bonding opportunities among individuals with similar extremist agenda across the globe.

Online radicalised individuals can be both active (those engaging in violent action), or passive. Passive radicalisation is found among individuals that do not have the intention of turning into violent jihadists, but contribute to spreading the message on the Internet.[14]

---

13 Nor Fadzila Adi Putra & Jamaludin Ibrahim, Online Radicalisation and Violent Extremism, Imperial Journal of Interdisciplinary Research (IJIR) Vol-3, Issue-11, 2017, https://www.onlinejournal.in/IJIRV3I11/103.pdf

14 Ibid

India's counter-radicalisation approach

Being close to the epicentre of modern jihadism in the Af-Pak region since its inception in the early 1980s, India can claim to have successfully withstood the virulent strain of Islamist terrorism and radicalisation constantly emanating from across its borders and only occasionally from within its large population.

However, as part of its journey toward becoming a major political and economic power on the global stage, India is presently undergoing major political and societal changes and its 172-million strong Muslim populace is also part of this massive process.

Given the complexities emanating from such a transformative stage, Indian Muslims have not been entirely immune to the threat of radical Islamist ideology and militancy. Still the country can be proud that its Muslim citisenry has in large numbers stood up against the insinuations of radical extremism and terror, and that incidents of jihadist violence have been remarkably low when compared to extremist Islamic violence afflicting several countries in West Asia, North Africa and the West in recent years.

In this regard, the deep-seated syncretism of Indian society and the cohesiveness of its community and family structures have played a vital role in withstanding the conspiracies of hate and sedition from waylaying its young population. It is perhaps for this reason that despite having the third largest Muslim population in the world, only a little over a hundred Indians are suspected to be members of the ISIS till date, while many countries in the West with much smaller Muslim populations have yielded militants affiliated to this group in their thousands.

However, the swamp of radicalisation continues to spew terrorist tentacles in the region which keeps India on guard and rightfully wary of the continuing threat, even as it maintains a tenuous balance wherein religious freedoms and sensitivities enshrined in Indian constitution are upheld without compromising on the imperatives of national security and social harmony.

In this respect, it is important to differentiate the process of

Islamist radicalisation in the state of Jammu and Kashmir from the rest of India. From the Indian perspective, the problem related to the state of Jammu and Kashmir is not caused by religious radicalisation per se, but is a politically motivated seditious campaign conducted by the state of Pakistan against the country — an unfortunate vestige of India's partition in 1947. Thus, the political and social dynamics of the Kashmir problem has more elements to it than conventional jihadist radicalisation.

In any case, the highly alert yet cautious approach of Indian security agencies in not over-reacting to the threat of radicalisation, and thereby going overboard in their response has proven to be a highly successful policy thus far.

In its counter-radicalisation campaigns, the effort of security agencies have been to isolate, localise and de-politicise operations so that the religious community does not feel being unduly targeted and becomes a willing contributor towards solving the relatively smaller incidents of terrorism.

Thus, Indian security agencies have so far engaged families of suspects, community leaders and elders, religious preachers and imams as well as civil society members in the process of counseling, apprehending, de-radicalizing and wherever possible rehabilitating suspects in order to contain the problem, without allowing sensitive matters to spiral out of control.[15]

Curiously, Indian security agencies have preferred to employ sociological approaches towards counter-radicalisation and have employed sociological, psychological and cultural means for defusing the problem without taking recourse to heavy handed security-centric measures.

As part of its de-radicalisation measures, Indian security agencies have initiated post-surrender and post-detention programs, such as:

---

15 Shweta Desai, 'India Turns to a Soft Approach to Prevent Radicalisation', Centre for Land Warfare Studies (CLAWS), 28 September 2015, available at http://www.claws.in/1443/india-turns-to-a-soft-approach-to-preventradicalisation-shweta-desai.html

a) ideological or religious counselling,

b) vocational education,

c) recreational and psychological rehab,

d) behavior modification programmes,

e) inter-religious or inter-communal discourse programs,

f) post-release surveillance and care, as well as

g) involvement of family members and civil society to foster rehabilitation etc.

From youth bulge to dividend

Indian policy makers have been looking into various new paradigms for developing more meaningful strategies against radicalisation. Schemes have been initiated for greater engagement with Muslim groups, religious and political organisations, civil society, educational centres (schools and colleges), research and social activist groups to launch counter-radicalisation and social harmony programmes.

Various prison programmes have been devised to prevent radicalisation, as well as to de-radicalise offenders etc. through religious and psychological counseling, vocational and other rehabilitation programmes. Greater inter-communal interaction through the hosting of Urdu and Hindi literary and poetic symposiums, sporting events etc. are being conducted. Inter-communal housing schemes to prevent the physical polarisation and ghettoisation of communities are also initiated.

The government has also started research for developing effective counter-narratives and strategic communications measures, as well as for formulating appropriate legislative measures.

However, there is room for improvement when it comes to tackling economic and social prejudice and inequalities, speedy dispensation of justice, as well as cracking down on the funding of certain radicalizing groups in the country. There is also a need for

a) launching counseling programmes for parents over raising their adolescents,

b) opening help lines for psychological counseling of the adolescents and teenagers,

c) providing career guidance and employment opportunities for the youth.

Apparently, there is historical evidence to prove the correlation between increase in youth population, also known (as youth bulges), which in sync with rapid urbanisation, has been a major contributor to political violence, especially in contexts of unemployment and poverty.

India's great economic success may have been one of the contributing factors in mitigating this deadly mix. With economic growth rates slowing down even in emerging markets in recent years, any reversal in the economic success story runs the risk of large number of educated young men becoming unemployed and increasingly frustrated, if not prone to violence.

Many Muslim youth in India found employment in Arab Gulf countries in recent decades. Although, their presence in these countries is often said to have increased the threat of radicalisation, it is possible that the economic prosperity of Indian Muslim expatriates in the Gulf may have mitigated their inclination towards extremism. With Gulf states increasingly nationalizing their jobs, the return of the Indian expats to the country might accentuate the problem of radicalisation and violent extremism in the future.

On a positive note, a large number of Muslim role models in every walk of life serve as beacons for young members of the community in the country to follow and emulate — be they political leaders, religious luminaries, Bollywood superstars, sporting celebrities, artistes, journalists, etc. Their success stories in a strong and secular India have helped Indian Muslims to remain committed to nation building and in keeping themselves away from divisive messaging emanating mainly from foreign sources.

Unlike Europe, Muslims have been part of the country for about a millennium and having recently gone through the purge of partition have stuck close to India's syncretic culture that is resilient against the threat of any global jihadist radicalisation. Having said that let us close with one of Shakespeare's cynical rants in *The Winter's Tale*, against the propensity of adolescents and the young to create mischief:

"I would there were no age between sixteen and three-and-twenty,

Or that youth would sleep out the rest;

for there is nothing in the between but getting wenches with child, wronging the ancientry, stealing, fighting."[16]

---

16 William Shakespeare, The Winter's Tale, Act 3, Scene 3, line 65

SECTION – V

Appraisal of Indo-Uzbek Relations and Way Forward - Uzbekistan's View

Prof. Mirzokhid Rakhimov

Uzbekistan and India have strong historical links. In modern times Uzbekistan and India established diplomatic and inter-state relations, and periodic exchanges of high-level visits, mutual agreements, and work towards further developing and strengthening bilateral relations. At present there are diversity of interests and multilateral relations in Central Asia. In the age of strategic uncertainties, India, Uzbekistan, Central and South Asia have opportunities to extend bilateral and multilateral partnership. Current and future Central Asian international relations will be prompted by the common threat linking the regional and global issues and challenges.

Dynamics of Uzbekistan and Indian bilateral relation

The start of the twenty-first century in the context of geopolitical changes in Central Asia has witnessed the involvement of a number of countries in the region with bilateral and multilateral approaches. Uzbekistan and India have strong historical and cultural links for centuries. During the Soviet times the Central Asian republics especially Uzbekistan had strong links with India and the first foreign visit of Uzbekistan President Islam Karimov was to Delhi in August 1991 just before disintegration of the Soviet Union.

On December 26, 1991, India was among the first to recognise the independence of the Republic of Uzbekistan, and on March 18, 1992, the Protocol on the Establishment of Diplomatic Relations was signed. Since then Uzbekistan and India periodically exchanges visits, inter-governmental commissions, foreign office consultations, working groups and other institutional mechanisms to systemically work towards further developing and strengthening bilateral relations.

Uzbekistan maintains regular political dialogue with India at the highest level. In April 2005 Islam Karimov paid a visit to India and during the meeting, the parties noted the consistent development of bilateral relations and fostered mutual cooperation. A year later in April 2006, the Prime Minister of India Manmohan Singh visited Uzbekistan. An exchange of views took place on further development of bilateral ties in the political, trade-economic, scientific-technical, cultural-humanitarian and other areas of cooperation, as well as regional and international issues of mutual interest.

In accordance with the changes taking place in the world, the sides stressed the relevance of the issues of reforming the structure and activities of the UN, increase its effectiveness in confronting the challenges and threats of modernity. During the visit of M. Singh at the Tashkent University of Information Technologies, the Indo-Uzbek Centre of Information Technologies named after late Indian PM Jawahar Lal Nehru was inaugurated.

In 2011, President of Uzbekistan Islam Karimov paid a state visit to India and several agreements were signed, including economic packet over $ 2.2 billion. The discussion also touched on the evolving situation in neighboring Afghanistan and reaffirmed the grave necessity for a soonest establishment of peace and stability in that country, one that would open up wider opportunities for regional cooperation and help institute and advance cost-effective routes reducing the distance between the markets of India and Central Asia. In this regard, the prospects emerging from setting up Central Asia-Persian Gulf land transport corridor as well as Trans-Afghan access strip have been telling.

In May 2013, the Vice-President of India Mohammad Hamid Ansari visited Tashkent and during the visit, the governmental delegations and private businesses of both countries discussed the trade and services, creation of mutually beneficial joint ventures in high-tech industries. During the exchange of views on the problem of

Afghanistan, it was noted that the stabilisation of the situation in this long-suffering country meets the interests of India and Uzbekistan and opens new prospects for deepening cooperation between the states of Central and South Asia.

On July 6, 2015, the Prime Minister of India Narendra Modi paid an official visit to the Republic of Uzbekistan. During the talks, the President of Uzbekistan and the Prime Minister of India held a broad exchange of views on issues of giving new impetus to Uzbek-Indian relations by tapping new opportunities, expanding the scale of cooperation in the political, economic, investment and cultural-humanitarian spheres. Narendra Modi highlighted that India considers Uzbekistan as one of its most reliable and important partner in Central Asia and the visit was a good opportunity to intensify bilateral relations and take them to the next level. The meeting also considered North-South corridor, regional and international issues.

In February 2017, newly elected Uzbek President Mirziyoyev initiated the Strategy for the Further Development of Uzbekistan 2017-2021.[1] The Strategy covers five main priorities, including implementing a balanced and constructive foreign policy, creating a security belt around Uzbekistan, achieving stability, and being in friendly relations with its neighboring countries.

On June 9, 2017, the President of Uzbekistan Shavkat Mirziyoyev, during the SCO summit in Astana, met the Indian PM Narendra Modi. During the meeting it was stressed that the sides attached special importance to the political dialogue, as well as continuing mutual support within the framework of international structures. The possibilities of joint implementation of projects in such areas as the development of joint software products, the sale of telecommunications equipment, the processing of fruit and vegetable products, silk and leather, the production of auto parts, electrical products, household chemicals and plant protection products were considered. The President of Uzbekistan congratulated the Prime Minister of India on the adoption of the decision at the SCO summit on India's joining the organisation as a full member. Narendra

---

1   http://lex.uz/pages/getpage.aspx?lact_id=3107042. (03.28.2017).

Modi noted that this historic event would create fundamentally new opportunities for the development of a multifaceted bilateral partnership and will expand practical regional cooperation in the fields of security, trade, economic and investment spheres.

Shavkat Mirziyoyev and Narendra Modi also met on June 9, 2018 during the SCO summit in Qingdao, where they reaffirmed the strong political will of the two countries to give a new momentum to the entire spectrum of bilateral relations.

The cooperation between Uzbekistan and India in the trade and economic area has seen a positive upsurge. The major import items from India are pharmaceutical products, organic chemicals, mechanical equipment, paper and cardboard, food products, optical instruments, tanning and dyeing extracts, etc. Indian business is particularly interested in the opportunities provided by the transcontinental intermodal hub at the city airport Navoi. Currently, this international hub has regular flights to industrial centres in India like Delhi and Mumbai.

Currently, Uzbekistan has more than 100 enterprises with the participation of Indian capital. According to the results of 2017, the trade turnover between the two countries increased by 15 per cent and amounted to $ 323,6 million. However, this indicator does not fully reflect the opportunities of the two countries, Uzbekistan and India have a huge potential for increasing the volume of mutual trade. Among the successful examples of cooperation is the production of auto parts with Minda in the free economic zone "Navoi", as well as the enterprises with Nofa Farm and Ultra Health Care companies in the production of drugs in the Surkhandarya and Tashkent region.

A major increase has been in the field of tourism. Indians visit the ancient cities of Tashkent, Samarkand, Bukhara with great interest. Every year the number of tourists from Uzbekistan visiting Delhi, Agra, Jaipur, Mumbai and other tourist spots has also increased.

The leading higher educational institutions and scientific institutes of Uzbekistan and India cooperate in various fields of educational and scientific activity, exchange faculty and students, and also cooperate in organising joint conferences, symposiums, seminars, and joint publication[2]. It should be noted that India is implementing a program of technical and economic cooperation in almost 160 countries around the world. Uzbekistan has been a member of the ITEC program since 1993. Every year, as part of this program, many Uzbek specialists raise their qualifications in prestigious universities in India in various areas, such as information technology, management, language courses, etc.[3]

Diversity and challenges of regionalism in Eurasia

The 21st century is witness to a new stage of geopolitical alignments started in Eurasia and the main actors increasingly compete with each other for gaining influence and space.

The Central Asian states were among the founding members of the Commonwealth of Independent States(CIS) in Alma-Ata on December 1991. The CIS is a platform for coordination by member countries but also an important tool for Russia to maintain its sphere of interest. Different agreements on economic, military, and political issues were signed at the summits of the CIS Council in 2009-2017. The most of it only exist on paper due to the structural limitations within the CIS. For example, the nine member-states, including the Central Asian states, signed Free Trade Zone Agreement within the CIS that cancelled duties, taxes and fees. However, in reality each country still follows its own customs procedures.

In autumn 2011, Vladimir Putin proposed creation of "Eurasian Union" and after his reelection in 2012, reformulated Russia's foreign policy. In May 2013 in Astana, the presidents of Russia, Belarus and Kazakhstan held a meeting of the Supreme Eurasian Economic Council and the main outcome was the decision to start the *Eurasian Economic Union* from January 2015. In 2015 Armenia and Kyrgyz Republic joined to the Eurasian Economic Union.

---

2   In particularly joint publications include: K.Warikoo, M.Rakhimov (eds). Uzbekistan Special.Journal *Himalayan and Central Asian Studies* (Uzbekistan Special). New Delhi. 2015. P.230; "South and Central Asia. Insights and Commentaries". Anita Sengupta, Mirzokhid Rakhimov (eds). New Delhi, Knowledge World, 2015. – 409 c.

3   Author of chapter was among who participated in ITEC program in 2002.

At present Kazakhstan, Kyrgyzstan and Tajikistan are members of Russia lead military alliance the *Collective Security Treaty Organisation* (CSTO).[4] However, within the CSTO's operations, a number of problems surfaced, wherein the member countries have expressed a variety of opinions and assessments of the status and prospects of cooperation.

In particular, in 2008, when Uzbekistan secured its CSTO membership, it refused to sign a number of documents of the CSTO, including the prohibition of opening up on the territory of a Member State of the CSTO without the consent of all members of the organisation. Uzbekistan also refused to participate in the creation of the Collective Rapid Reaction Forces, and has not signed the agreement on the participation of national military forces in the fight against possible internal conflicts in some of the CSTO member states. As a result, in 2012, Uzbekistan officially announced its withdrawal from the CSTO; it was however only suspended by the organisation.

China, one of the largest neighbors of the region has prioritised the expansion of political and economic relations based on multilateral cooperation as its policy for Central Asia. In particular, in 1996 Russia, China, Kazakhstan, Kyrgyzstan, and Tajikistan established the "Shanghai Five". In 2001 with Uzbekistan's participation the *Shanghai Cooperation Organisation* (SCO) as established. The SCO passed through a number of interesting phases in its institutional and political evolution and at present represents an international instrument to coordinate areas of multilateral cooperation. At present Mongolia, Iran, Afghanistan and Belarus have observers' status, while Turkey, Armenia, Azerbaijan, Cambodia and Nepal are dialogue-country partners. India and Pakistan commenced their membership process at the SCO summit in June 2016 in Tashkent and in June 2017 in Astana meeting got full membership, which

---

4   CSTO was created on the basis of the Collective Security Treaty signed in May 1992 and includes Armenia, Kasakhstan, Kyrgyzstan, Russia, Tajikistan and Uzbekistan. Then he was joined by Azerbaijan, Georgia and Belarus. The Treaty entered into force in 1994, but in 1999, Uzbekistan, Azerbaijan and Georgia have refused his prolongation membership. In 2006, Uzbekistan has restored its membership in the CSTO.

significantly expanded the organisation. However, it should be noted that the differences between the SCO member states on a number of political and economic aspects, in addition to the expansion of the organisation brings new challenges and problems for the SCO.

In 2013, Chinese President Xi announced creation "The Silk Road Economic Belt" Jinping in Astana, and in 2014 the Silk Road Fund (50 billion USD) was established, and in 2016 Asian Infrastructure Investment Bank (AIIB) (more 100 billion USD) was established with aim to provide investment and financial support to cooperation in infrastructure, resources, industry, finance sector as well as other transport communication projects involving various countries. Central Asian republics expressed their support for the mega project and were among the cofounders of the AIIB. But there are many challenges to the stability and sustainable development of partner countries in Belt and Road Initiative. These require comprehensive economic, political and security cooperation at bilateral and multilateral cooperation. In Central Asia it is needed not only for the realisation of the regional and international projects, increasing connectivity and technological development, but also for the cooperation between 'Belt and Road' participating countries including high-tech, innovations, education, public diplomacy and tourism.

During its EU presidency in 2007, Germany initiated process for increasing bilateral and multilateral partnership with Central Asian states leading to new *EU strategy toward Central Asia* 2007-2013 being accepted[5]. In 2014 the EU decided to extend the strategy for another five years committing a further one billion Euros, the same as for 2007-2013. At present along with Russia and China, the EU is the main trading partner of Central Asia, especially for Kazakhstan. The EU is keen to tap energy resources from Central Asia. In coming decades EU plans to extend its external energy supplies[6]. Central Asian states are also keen on for alternative corridors for resource export like the Transport corridor Europe - Asia (TRACECA) trade

---

5   The EU and Central Asia: Strategy for a new partnership. http://register. consilium.europa.eu/pdf/en.

6   BP Energy Outlook 2035. January 2014.

corridor between Asia and Europe[7]. However, for the complete realisation of this idea, there are certain difficulties in formulating a common policy of the states through which the route passes, and the positions of various countries.

For the Central Asian states relations with the USA are important in the context of cooperation with the developed countries of the West. In 2011, US Secretary of State Hillary Clinton unveiled the 'New Silk Road' policy, which involves the creation of infrastructure linking Central Asia and South Asia through Afghanistan, and trade liberalisation between the two regions. But, neither the private US organisations, nor the US Government is investing enough to overcome the economic, political challenges, nor talk of the new Silk Road remains just that – talk, since the funding for it has not been allocated.[8]

Since 1992 the United States has been the only major external actor in Central Asia, but without a regular consultative multilateral mechanism. In November 2015 US Secretary of State John Kerry paid visits to the countries of Central Asia and met with Presidents of Uzbekistan, Kazakhstan, Kyrgyzstan, Tajikistan and Turkmenistan to discuss bilateral relations and regional stability issues. In Samarkand Secretary Kerry and Foreign Ministers of Kazakhstan, Kyrgyzstan, Tajikistan, Turkmenistan and Uzbekistan had a meeting under the agesis of the new cooperation format "Central Asia+USA" ("C5+1"). The "C5+1" Joint Declaration of Partnership and Cooperation, included regional trade, transport and communication, business climate in the region, environmental sustainability challenges, cooperation to prevent and counter trans boundary threats and challenges, support Afghanistan, and others.[9]

Shortly after the Samarkand meeting that the U.S. Assistance

---

7   The EU and Central Asia: Strategy for a New Partnership // The Permanent Representatives Committee. 31 May 2007. P.10.

8   Stephen Blank, "Introduction" in Stephen Blank (ed.), *Central Asia after 2014* (The US Army War College, 2013), 7.

9   Joint Declaration of Partnership and Cooperation by the Five Countries of Central Asia and The United States of America, Samarkand, Uzbekistan. http://www.state.gov/r/pa/prs/ps/2015/11/249050.htm.

to Central Asia was announced, it includes: Competitiveness, Training, and Jobs; Central Asia Trade Forums; Climate Adaptation and Mitigation Program for the Aral Sea Basin; Smart Waters and others.[10] But the success of C5+1 in the issues raised require specific and long-term projects and programs implementation between members.

The start of the 21st century saw the activation of bilateral and multilateral approaches of Japan in Eurasia. In 1997 Japan formulated the "Silk Road" Diplomacy policy toward the region and in two decades Japan and Central Asian bilateral political, economic and multilateral relations has increased considerably. Japan allotted soft loans and commercial credits totaling more than 3.5 billion USD, which were aimed at projects for the development of telecommunication networks, renovation of the repair-and-construction of plants, modernisation of airports, railways system, as well as energy. Japanese Prime Ministers Koizumi and Abe in 2006 and 2015 respectively visited the Central Asian states to enhance its relations with region. In 2004 Japan and Central Asia established a multilateral framework *"Central Asia plus Japan."* Its main concepts were coordination and cooperation. It needs constant dialogue meetings, full scale implementation of projects as well as expanding the range of cooperation for it to be successful.

Another leading economic partner of the Central Asia countries, especially for Uzbekistan, is the Republic of Korea[11]. In 2007 *"Republic of Korea – Central Asia"* discussion forum was organised. In the period between 2007-2017 under the charter "Republic of Korea – Central Asia" meetings were held in South Korea as well as in the Central Asian republics for strengthening and developing cooperation in various spheres, including IT sector, agriculture, medicine and health, "E-government", energy-

---

10 New U.S. Assistance Programs in Central Asia. http://www.state.gov/r/pa/prs/ps/2015/11/249051.htm.

11 Mirzokhid Rakhimov. Uzbekistan and South Korea: toward special relationship // CACI Analyst. John Hopkins University. USA. June 10, 2016. http://www.cacianalyst.org/publications/analytical-articles/item/13369-uzbekistan-and-south-korea-towards-a-special-relationship.html.

effectiveness and natural recourses, construction and infrastructure, science and technologies, finances, textile. It may be noted that much like India, due to similarities of national identities of Korean and Central Asians, Korean cinema, cartoons and music are also very popular in the region.

India and Uzbekistan in a broader partnership

The contemporary Central Asian states consider it important to develop communication networks from the East to the West, and from the South to the North. The Central Asian republics are keen to develop new arteries connecting Europe and Asia, including the TRACECA. In 2007, EU launched "The reorganisation of transport network by advancing Rail Freight Concepts (RETRACK)" to identify main competing overland railway corridor between Europe and China.

China has been actively developing new connectivites in Eurasia, particularly to Europe. Its branch goes to the north-west and south-west directions; the first passing through Russia, Ukraine, Belarus, Poland and other countries, and the second through Kazakhstan, Uzbekistan, Turkmenistan, Iran, Turkey and Europe. The construction of the Tashkent-Andizhan-Osh-Sarytash-Irkeshtam motor highway and the railway project Kashgar-Osh-Andizhan are considered as a part of the intensive economic exchange between the China and Central Asia. But during the last ten years China – Kyrgyzstan–Uzbekistan rail project implementation has been facing certain difficulties in formulating a common policy for the states through which it passes. The building of railroad Angren (Tashkent region) – Pap (Namangan region in Ferghana valley) on the territory of Uzbekistan could also be considered. But there are considerable challenges in the Ferghana Valley, including tapping Tajikistan's transit potential. There is also the issue of transportation of hydrocarbons from Central Asia and the Caspian region to external markets. In 2005, the oil pipeline from Atasu (Kazakhstan) to Alashankou (China) was completed, in 2009 the first gas pipeline (A line) between Central Asia-China was constructed, and in the following years B and C lines which pass through the territories of Turkmenistan, Uzbekistan, and Kazakhstan, was completed.

Stabilisation and positive changes in Afghanistan would open up new opportunities for Central and South Asian cooperation. Since 2002 the Central Asian countries have been actively have been participating in the reconstruction and rebuilding of the country. In particular, Tajikistan and Uzbekistan electricity export to Afghanistan; in addition Uzbekistan has built a number of bridges, highways and railway lines in the country. With financial support of Asian Development Bank in 2011 Uzbekistan constructed the railway line Khairaton-Mazar-e-Sharif, and currently the Mazar-e-Sharif-Herat railway is under construction. In March 2018 with Uzbek President Mirziyoyev and Afghan President Ghani held the Tashkent Conference on Afghanistan "Peace process, security cooperation and regional connectivity". Kazakhstan is exporting wheat and other goods and carries out different educational project in Kazakhstan for Afghan students. India has contributed more than two billion USD support for reconstruction and different educational and social programs in Afghanistan. Further, an intergovernmental agreement on the construction of the pipeline Turkmenistan-Afghanistan-Pakistan-India (TAPI) was signed. Uzbekistan could join to TAPI. The improvement of transport connections between Central Asia and Afghanistan would be a significant contribution toward the future economic recovery of Afghanistan, and also contributed towards the development of transport communications of Central Asia countries with the South and East Asia.

The end of the twentieth century was characterised by significant geopolitical changes and transformation in Asia. The Central Asian states voiced their interest in developing mutually beneficial relations with different Asian regions and leading countries like Japan, Republic of Korea, India, Turkey, Iran and others. Today in Central and South Asian cooperation the role of India is very important and India has expressed its keen interest in actualisation of the North-South trade corridor, and enhancing trade, and energy security.[12] Improvements of India-Pakistan, as well as Afghan-Pakistan relations would be an important factor in connecting South and Central Asia. In 2017 India and Pakistan got full membership in the SCO and it is for the first time since 2001 when the organisation expanded its membership. There are challenges, but also opportunities for Central Asia's cooperation with South Asia and other regions of the world.

On June 22, 2018, the UN General Assembly adopted the resolution on "Strengthening regional and international cooperation to ensure peace, stability and sustainable development in the Central Asian Region". The resolution calls on the international community, in particular the specialised agencies, funds and programs of the UN system, to support the priority areas of regional cooperation, integration and sustainable development in Central Asia, as determined by the countries of the region themselves[13].

For wider international cooperation an active dialogue and cooperation between the major and emerging powers is necessary. Central Asia's partnership with leading nations and international institutions is important for transformation and internationalising of the region. Strong regional and trans-regional cooperation will considerably contribute to the development of trade, economy and investment.

Conclusion

Since ancient time, Uzbekistan- India relations, as well as Central and South Asia have evolved through complex process of transformation. It is well known that there have been multiple paths to the modern world and it is accepted that there is no single development path to the modern world[14]. It is essential for Central Asian republics

---

12 See. Gulshan Sachdeva, *India in reconnecting Eurasia (*CISS, Washington DC, 2016).

13 https://www.un.org/press/en/2018/ga12030.doc.htm; https://mfa.uz/en/press/ statements/2018/06/15222

14 J.Kopstein and M.Lichbach. What us comparative politics? In J.Kopstein and M.Lichbach (ed.) *Comparative politics.Interests.Identities and institutions in*

to continue economic reforms, political liberalisation and regional cooperation with the support of the international community. Currently Uzbekistan is in the process of modernisation and liberalisation and Indian experience in this field is very relevant for Uzbekistan and whole of Central Asia, considering that in the last few decades India has made substantial progress in these aspects.

It is the fourth largest economy based on purchasing power, one of the largest food manufacturers that possesses diversified and extensive industrial base capable to compete. Indian companies are major players at the international level in spheres of marketing, production, purchasing, research and development. India is also a leading country in the sphere of IT and is the fourth largest pharmaceutical industry in the world.

Since 1991, Uzbekistan and India have established strong bilateral relations, though there are many challenges in the relations, wherein the absence of connectivity has been a major obstacle in developing economic and trade ties between India and whole Central Asia. The existing flights from Almaty, Ashgabat and Tashkent have the potential for expansion in terms of capacities and frequency. The tourist flow and movement of people would also benefit from this.

Regional cooperation and integration are among the most important trends in contemporary international relations. There are challenges, similarities and contradiction of multilateral relations in Central Asia (such as CIS, CSTO, EEU, SCO, Economic belt of Silk Road, C5+1, the EU strategy, Central Asia plus Japan, Central Asia – Republic of Korea and others). Descriptions and explanations must take into account particular local and regional situations, the internal and regional economies, cultures, and politics, and the transformations affected by the competitive international environment. Current and future Central Asian transformation would be governed by interlinked local, regional, trans-regional and global issues and challenges. In more than 25 years Central Asian states have created a more or less efficient system of checks and balances,

---

*a changing global order (*Cambridge University Press, 2009), 30.

in which none of the external actors is in a dominant position which would allow him to shape the countries' fates.

Central Asia participated in developing new links to the East and West, South and North. There are potentials for regional and trans-regional trade development which will facilitate foreign investment. Strong regional connectivity will contribute to global interdependence.

For enhancing Uzbek-India as well as South and Central Asia partnership it is necessary to achieve the following:

First, it is necessary to deepen reforms in the sphere of research and higher education, and to strengthen university autonomy and integrate Central Asian science with the international system. Uzbekistan and India need to enlarge strong educational partnership, academic cooperation and joint projects, which include joint lecture courses, textbooks, seminars and publications. It is important to extend public diplomacy, cultural links, and people to people as well as virtual partnership in the region.

Second, strong political and economic dialogue in Central Asia for the gradual development of institutional framework for the trans-regional cooperation. Uzbekistan and India could work on further diversification of their economy, the expansion of the private sector, attraction of foreign investment, and widespread adoption of renewable energy.

Third, development of regional and international transport connectivity is interlinked with the growth of economy and international tourism in Central and South Asia. For progress in this field, it is necessary to establish new routes with attendant infrastructure and service.

Fourth, stabilisation of Afghanistan is important for Central Asia. International community needs to have joint projects for Afghanistan and Central Asia with neighboring countries' partnership.

To conclude, strong Uzbek-India international partnership is needed for democratic and economic reforms, a new technology, innovation and attracting foreign investment. The international community's support for Central Asian republics will contribute to the maintenance stability in modernisations of the region.

Appraisal of Indo-Uzbek Relations and The Way Forward

Amb Skand Tayal

Relations between the Indian sub-continent and the present territory of Uzbekistan are ancient and civilisational. The region east of the river Oxus and cities of Bukhara, Samarkand, Kokand and Khiva were on the famed Silk Route and monks and merchants travelled to this region from areas around the Indus River and the Indo-Gangetic plain. Buddhism traveled from India through present day Afghanistan and Central Asia to China and further East. The Soviets followed by Uzbeks after 1990s have excavated and preserved the Buddhist archaeological sites in and around Termez. Bukhara and Samarkand had 'sarais' for Indian traders till the early 20th century and in Kokand there was also a crematorium for Hindus. [1]

In the Soviet period post consolidation of Communist Party of the Soviet Union (CPSU) hold on Central Asia and after the Second World War, Tashkent was promoted as a centre for interaction with South and East Asia. The present 'Tashkent State Institute of Oriental Studies' was founded as early as in 1918 with the name 'Turkistan Institute of Oriental Studies'. [2] After India gained independence in 1947 it emerged as a strong centre for study of Indian history, culture and languages including Hindi, Urdu, Bangla, Tamil etc. In 2006, India established a 'Mahatma Gandhi Centre for Indian Studies' at this Institute. [3]

---

1   Rhie, Marylin Martin. "Early Buddhist Art of China and Central Asia, Volume 3." 2010.

2   About Institute. Tashkent State Institute of Oriental Studies. Accessed August 14, 2018. http://tashgiv.uz/en/institut-haqida/.

3   Akbarov, Aslam. "Uzbekistan: 25 Years of Independence – the Model Strives

During the Soviet times, Tashkent was an important destination for Indian dignitaries. Prime Minister Jawaharlal Nehru's first visit to Uzbek SSR in 1955 is still remembered for the public adulation he received from the Uzbek masses. [4] Some poignant memories are also associated with Tashkent as the then Prime Minister Lal Bahadur Shastri passed away in Tashkent on 11 January 1966 after signing the Tashkent Agreement with Pakistan.[5]

Even after Uzbekistan's independence the city of Tashkent maintains a garden around the bust of late Prime Minister Shastri; also there is a street named after Smt Indira Gandhi. In the 1970s, there were scores of Uzbek girls who were named 'Indira' in the heydays of Indo-Soviet friendship.

Recognizing the importance of the Uzbek SSR as the centre of Central Asian culture, India had opened a consulate in Tashkent in 1987 which was quickly upgraded to a full Embassy after Uzbekistan became a sovereign Republic in 1992.[6]

Ever since the Central Asian Republics (CARs) declared their emergence as sovereign nations in 1991 in the aftermath of the collapse of the Soviet Union, India has paid great emphasis on the development of relations with all five CARs, particularly with Uzbekistan. This is both because of the centrality of Uzbekistan in the strategic, civilisational and economic evolution of the Central Asian region and the country's strong leadership.

Uzbekistan is a nation with a population of 32.1 million, which is more than half of the population of all the five CARs taken together.

on. The Economic Times. September 01, 2016. Accessed August 14, 2018. https://economictimes.indiatimes.com/news/politics-and-nation/uzbekistan-25-years-of-independence-the-model-strives-on/articleshow/53960381.cms.

4 Haidar, Suhasini. "Nehru's Soviet Sojourn." The Hindu. July 11, 2015. Accessed August 14, 2018. https://www.thehindu.com/features/magazine/nehrus-soviet-sojourn/article7407454.ece.

5 Britannica, The Editors of Encyclopaedia. "Tashkent Agreement." Encyclopædia Britannica. April 17, 2016. Accessed August 14, 2018. https://www.britannica.com/event/Tashkent-Agreement.

6 Embassy /High Commission /Consulate General of India. Accessed August 14, 2018. https://eoi.gov.in/tashkent/?2615?000.

[7] It is a double landlocked country with a total land boundary of 6,813 KM. It shares borders with five countries, Afghanistan (144 Km), Kazakhstan (2,300 Km), Kyrgyzstan (1,315 km), Tajikistan (1,312km) and Turkmenistan (1,793 km). [8] 80 per cent of the fertile Fergana valley- cradle of central Asian civilisation and culture-lies in Uzbekistan. [9] The ethnic distribution in the country is Uzbek (80 per cent), Russian (5.5 per cent), Tajik (5 per cent) and Kazakh (3 per cent). [10]

Uzbekistan is a secular, unitary, constitutional democratic Republic with several political parties. It has strong Presidential system of Government. Uzbekistan is active in multilateral fora e.g. Commonwealth of Independent States (CIS), Organisation for Security and Co-operation in Europe (OSCE), United Nations (UN), and the Shanghai Cooperation Organisation (SCO). After the death of the first President Islam Karimov with 27 years at the helm, former Prime Minister Shavkat Mirzioyev was elected President in 2016 with 88.6per cent vote in a multi-cornered contest. [11] The Uzbek polity and internal political structures are remarkably strong, stable and united. President Shavkat Mirzioyev has now charted a new course for Uzbekistan based on the firm foundations laid by his predecessor. The new administration has taken steps to reduce country's dependence on cotton, ease foreign travel, introduce tax reforms, establish realistic foreign exchange rates and make the

---

7 "Demographic Situation in the Republic Of Uzbekistan." Statistika Qo'mitasi - MAIN. Accessed August 14, 2018. https://www.stat.uz/en/435-analiticheskie-materialy-en1/2075-demographic-situation-in-the-republic-of-uzbekistan.

8 "Where Is Uzbekistan?" GraphicMaps. January 17, 2018. Accessed August 14, 2018. https://www.graphicmaps.com/uzbekistan.

9 "The Fergana Valley – at the Heart of Central Asia." Links-dar.org. April 20, 2017. Accessed August 14, 2018. https://links-dar.org/2015/08/23/the-fergana-valley-at-the-heart-of-central-asia/.

10 "Uzbekistan Population 2018." (Demographics, Maps, Graphs). Accessed August 14, 2018. http://worldpopulationreview.com/countries/uzbekistan-population/.

11 «Uzbekistan Replaces One Strongman with Another.» The Economist. December 10, 2016. Accessed August 14, 2018. https://www.economist.com/asia/2016/12/10/uzbekistan-replaces-one-strongman-with-another.

economy more open and transparent. [12]

Recognizing the cultural, economic and strategic importance of Uzbekistan, the then Prime Minister PV Narasimha Rao visited Tashkent on 23-25 May 1993. During the visit a treaty on the principles of inter-state relations and cooperation was signed laying the foundation of future friendly relations between the two countries. This agreement sets out the principles for bilateral relations by promising to develop relations in political, economic trade, science, technology and other fields. India also established an 'India Chair' in the World University of Economics and Diplomacy in Tashkent. [13] 50 scholarships under the prestigious Indian Technical and Economic Cooperation (ITEC) program were also offered. This number has now gone up to 130 and the scholarships are very much sought after by Uzbek professionals. [14]

Since the very beginning President Islam Karimov gave very high priority to relations with India and visited India in 1991, 1994, 2000, 2005 and in May 2011. [15] Prime Minister Dr Manmohan Singh visited Tashkent for a bilateral visit in 2006 and Prime Minister Narendra Modi in 2015. [16]

In the initial years of consolidation of the Uzbek state in the 1990s the emphasis in Indo-Uzbek bilateral relations was more on economic and cultural cooperation. [17]After attaining independence Uzbek leadership looked towards India for investments and rapid economic development. Unfortunately, at that time India was going

---

12 Raposa, Kenneth. "Eurasia's Latest Economic Reboot Can Be Found In Uzbekistan." Forbes. September 14, 2017. Accessed August 16, 2018. https://www.forbes.com/sites/kenraposa/2017/09/14/eurasias-new-perestroika-uzbekistan-silk-road-china/#162c08af6f25.

13 Indian Council for Cultural Relations | Government of India. Accessed August 16, 2018. http://iccr.gov.in/content/lal-bahadur-shastri-centre-indian-culture-tashkent.

14 Indo-Uzbekistan Relations, Ministry of External Affairs http://mea.gov.in/Portal/ForeignRelation/Uzbekistan_July_2016.pdf

15 Ibid

16 Ibid

17 Ibid

through an economic crisis and a foreign exchange crunch. The Indian economy was in the process of a paradigm change from a regulated socialist economy to a more liberal and open economy, India therefore missed the opportunity for a deeper economic engagement with Uzbekistan ceding space to other countries like Republic of Korea. [18] The Government of India had opened generous lines of credit through EXIM Bank to support Indian investors establishing factories in Uzbekistan. But many of such investments turned bad, thereby showing the Indian business in poor light.

Trade relations between India and Uzbekistan are governed by the Agreement on Trade and Economic Cooperation signed in May 1993. [19] India and Uzbekistan have signed an Agreement on Avoidance of Double Taxation in 1993 and one for Bilateral Investment Promotion and Protection in May 1999. [20] There is an Indo-Uzbek Inter-government Commission on Trade, Economic, and Scientific and Technological Cooperation headed by the Commerce Minister on India's side which has met ten times with last meeting in 2014. [21]

Indo-Uzbek bilateral trade has grown rapidly rising from about $20 million in 2012 to $ 323 million in 2017. India's exports to Uzbekistan in 2017 were $291 million and import from Uzbekistan $33 million. [22] India's export basket mainly constitutes of pharmaceutical products, mechanical equipment, vehicle parts, optical equipment etc. India imports fruits and vegetables products, services, fertilizers and lubricants etc. from Uzbekistan. [23]

---

18 Rakhimov, Mirzokhid, and Sung Dong Ki. "Uzbekistan and South Korea: Towards a Special Relationship." The CACI Analyst. June 10, 2016. Accessed August 16, 2018. https://www.cacianalyst.org/publications/analytical-articles/item/13369-uzbekistan-and-south-korea-towards-a-special-relationship.html.

19 Indo-Uzbekistan Relations, Ministry of External Affairs http://mea.gov.in/Portal/ForeignRelation/Uzbekistan_July_2016.pdf

20 Ibid

21 Embassy /High Commission /Consulate General of India. Accessed August 16, 2018. https://eoi.gov.in/tashkent/?2615?000.

22 Ibid

23 Ibid

According to Uzbek statistics, 113 companies created with participation of Indian capital are working in Uzbekistan, out of which 19 companies are with 100 per cent Indian investments, a major success since the poor show in the 90s. India's major investments include the Ashok Minda Group's investment of about $5 million in Navoi Free Economic Zone which is producing automobile components for General Motors in Uzbekistan. Fun and Food Village, Gurgaon has invested $ 4 million in 2011 to set up an Amusement Park. Nova Pharma is in a Joint Venture based in Termez city with an investment of $8 million to manufacture pharmaceutical and healthcare products. BRAVO Pharma with an investment of $5.5 million, Ramada Hotel in Tashkent, Shayana Pharma and Orion Medicity are other important investments from India. [24]

India is a preferred destination for medical treatment of Uzbek dignitaries and citizens. Orion Medicity is affiliated with 'Medanta the Medcity' in India. It is opined that about 8000 Uzbeks visit India annually for medical treatment and that this number is growing by about 10 per cent each year.

Uzbekistan is rich in cotton and there have been projects for manufacture of yarn and cloth in Uzbekistan. An $81 million investment by the Spentex Industries Ltd in 'Spentex Tashkent Toytepa Tekstil' textile mill in Tashkent[25] has not been successful but another investment in this sector through Indorama textiles in Kokand Textile Mills has been doing well[26]. Spentex had amalgamated Indorama Textiles with in Jan 2007. For importers of Indian products, particularly in pharmaceutical sector, the restrictions on repatriation of their earnings and purchase costs from

---

24 Ibid

25 "Spentex Buys Uzbek Co for $81m." The Economic Times. July 25, 2006. Accessed September 03, 2018. https://economictimes.indiatimes.com/ industry/cons-products/garments-/-textiles/spentex-buys-uzbek-co-for-81m/ articleshow/1803100.cms.

26 "Indorama Buys Bankrupt Uzbek Cotton Mill." Clothesource. July 06, 2010. Accessed September 03, 2018. https://www.clothesource.net/indorama-buys-bankrupt-uzbek-cotton-mill/.

Uzbekistan has been a persistent problem hampering bilateral trade. However, under President Shavkat Mirziyoyev's leadership Uzbek government has relaxed its control over foreign exchange valuation and repatriation and this is likely to improve the situation. [27]

At the request of the Uzbek Government, India has paid special attention to the development of human resources and skills in Uzbekistan. India offers 130 scholarships to Uzbek professionals under its' Indian Technical and Economic Cooperation' Program (ITEC) which are very much in demand. Under this program India bears the full cost including travel of Uzbek teachers, civil servants and experts in various fields ranging from banking and accounting to agriculture and English language.

India established the 'Jawaharlal Nehru Indo-Uzbek Centre for Information Technology' in Tashkent in 2006 with a grant of Rupees 3 Crores. This centre was inaugurated by the then Prime Minister Dr Manmohan Singh during his state visit to Uzbekistan in 2006. In October 2011, under a Joint Action Plan formulated to promote the activities of the centre, Rupees 4.2 Crores were spent by India's Ministry of External Affairs. After the up gradation was completed in 2014, the centre is functioning very well. [28]

Uzbek and Indian IT companies are exploring the possibility of establishing Joint Ventures to provide IT services to Russian and Kazakh markets. India's known expertise in software development coupled with Russian language skills of Uzbek IT professionals would be in a position to offer outsourcing solutions to Russian and Kazakh corporations, banks, airlines, municipal governments etc. However, issues like independent and reliable communication channels and confidentiality of data transferred would need to

---

27 Mamatkulov, Mukhammadsharif. "Uzbeks Queue to Buy, Sell Dollars as Soviet-era Restrictions Lifted." Reuters. September 05, 2017. Accessed August 16, 2018. https://www.reuters.com/article/us-uzbekistan-forex-reform/uzbeks-queue-to-buy-sell-dollars-as-soviet-era-restrictions-lifted-idUSKCN1BG1V4.

28 Indo-Uzbekistan Relations, Ministry of External Affairs http://mea.gov.in/Portal/ForeignRelation/Uzbekistan_July_2016.pdf

be resolved satisfactorily. This could be a promising new area of bilateral collaboration and would help generate employment both in Uzbekistan and India.

During the important visit of Prime Minister Dr Manmohan Singh to Tashkent in 2006- an Indian Prime Minister's visit after a gap of 13 years- several important MoUs had been signed, one MoU was for establishing the Uzbekistan-India Entrepreneurship Development Centre (EDC) in Tashkent. The objective of the centre is to set up collaboration in exchange of experience in the field of small and private enterprises to assist in the economic development of Uzbekistan. With a grant of Rupees 3.35 Crores, the feasibility study has been completed by the Entrepreneurship Development Institute of India in Ahmedabad. The premises for the centre have been finalised by the Uzbek Government and the Centre is expected to be functional soon. [29]

India's endeavor has been to work with the Uzbek Government for capacity building so that Uzbek entrepreneurs learn the skills to establish small and medium scale industry. Uzbekistan has a rising population of educated youth who need to be gainfully employed. In this context the enthusiastic embrace of the Chinese 'Belt and Road Initiative' by Uzbekistan is puzzling. It is for Uzbek policy makers to examine whether any Uzbek manufactured goods will be exported in either direction on these new roads. These new railway and roads would make the Chinese product even cheaper in the Uzbek markets and adversely impact the cost competitiveness of Uzbekistan manufactured goods. This is a serious policy issue and the virtues of un-fettered free trade are being re-examined by many countries including India particularly when one party does not sincerely adhere to the accepted rules of trade.

On 6-7 July 2015 Prime Minister Narendra Modi visited Tashkent as part of his outreach to all the five CARs. During this visit of Prime Minister Narendra Modi and the former President

---

29 Embassy /High Commission /Consulate General of India. Accessed August 16, 2018. https://eoi.gov.in/tashkent/?2615?000.

Islam Karimov called for more security cooperation and to further expand and strengthen bilateral relations. A MoU on Cyber Security was also signed during the visit. Prime Minister Modi visited Tashkent again on 23-24 June 2016 to attend the Summit meeting of Shanghai Cooperation Organisation during which India signed the Memorandum of Obligations for obtaining status of the Member State of SCO.[30]

A high level multi-sectorial delegation led by Uzbek Minister of Foreign Affairs Abdulaziz Kamilov visited India on 21-23 August 2017. The high powered delegation included Minister of Foreign Trade Elyor Ganiyev and senior officials from several ministries. Minister Kamilov had meetings with External Affairs Minister, Commerce Minister and National Security Advisor. At the Uzbek-India Business Forum held on 22 August 2017,22 contracts worth over $70 million were signed. [31]

Foreign Office Consultations are held regularly and the last round was held in March 2017 in Delhi. Uzbek diplomats are regularly trained in India's Foreign Service Institute. Twinning of Agra and Samarkand has been proposed and a draft MoU is under consideration of the two sides. There is considerable similarity in the architecture of the two medieval era cities. Recently, there are reports that artisans from Agra worked on the monument of late President Islam Karimov in Samarkand and that marble and stones were also sourced from India.

India and Uzbekistan are also building a defense relationship with training of Uzbek defense officers in India. During his visit to Tashkent in March 2018, Minister of state Shri M.J. Akbar had met the Uzbek Defense Minister and discussed the possibility of expanding defence partnership. Reportedly, Uzbekistan has offered India space to set up a defence manufacturing unit which could take the Indo-Uzbek relations to a qualitatively higher level. [32] It may

---

30 Ibid

31 Ibid

32 Chaudhury, Dipanjan Roy. "Uzbekistan Offers India Space for Defence Unit."

be recalled that in the 1990s and early 2000, India had purchased Ilyushin -76 platforms for India's AWACS. India's Ilyushin transport planes were also serviced and refurbished at the Tashkent Aircraft Production Organisation. [33]

India and Uzbekistan share common perceptions for ensuring regional peace and stability. At an ideological level the threat to both South Asia and Central Asia emanates from religious fundamentalism and danger of terrorism. Both the countries have been sharing intelligence about the terrorist groups and movement of individual terrorists. The concerned officials of the two sides meet regularly under the auspices of a joint working group on terrorism. [34]

The people of India and Uzbekistan recognise and cherish a deep cultural bond. Both the societies believe in strong family values blending tradition with a modern outlook. Bollywood films are very popular in all corners of Uzbekistan and no wedding is complete without Bollywood dances on Indian film music.

The popularity of Late Raj Kapoor and the Kapoor family in Uzbekistan is legendary. Raj Kapoor's famous films like Sangam, Bobby etc are shown regularly, and there is no Uzbek Orchestra which does not have the old time classic of the 1950s 'Awara Hoon' in its repertoire. In collaboration with the Uzbek Government, the Indian Embassy had organised a tour of the sons of Late Shri Raj Kapoor- Randhir Kapoor and Rishi Kapoor to Uzbekistan in 2007. The two eminent actors were accompanied by Shri Nitin Mukesh and a music group. The team was treated as state guests and all the public appearances drew massive crowds. At present stars like

The Economic Times. March 29, 2018. Accessed August 16, 2018. https:// economictimes.indiatimes.com/news/defence/uzbekistan-offers-india-space-for-defence-unit/articleshow/63525828.cms.

33 Pike, John. "Military." Vietnam War - American Return to Dog Fighting. Accessed August 16, 2018. https://www.globalsecurity.org/military/world/russia/chkalov.htm.

34 "India, Uzbekistan Ink Pacts to Boost Cooperation." The Hindu. April 03, 2016. Accessed August 16, 2018. https://www.thehindu.com/news/national/prime-minister-narendra-modis-visit-to-uzbekistan/article7392482.ece.

Amitabh Bachchan, the three Khans, Hema Malini and Aishwarya Rai are house hold names in Uzbekistan. The Indian film industry has generated a lot of good will for India in the hearts and minds of ordinary Uzbekistan people.

A 'Lal Bahadur Shastri Centre for Indian Culture' is being run by the Indian Council of Cultural Relations in Tashkent since 1995. [35] Its programs are very popular and it holds regular classes in Hindi, Kathak, and Yoga etc. Three Uzbek educational institutions teach Hindi and Indian culture, from primary to post-graduate level. Twenty five scholarships are being offered to Uzbekistan annually for various courses in Indian universities under ICCR, scholarship program and one scholarship for study of Hindi at the 'Kendriya Hindi Sansthan' of Agra.[36]

A landmark protocol on cooperation in the field of mass media had been signed in 1992 during the visit of the then President Islam Karimov. This protocol was upgraded in 2000 envisaging exchange of TV programs, visits of journalists, participation in international film festivals, cooperation among the films makers of both feature films and documentaries, visit of Radio and TV personnel etc. Uzbek Radio completed 50 years of Hindi broadcasting in 2012. Uzbek TV channels regularly show Indian films and serials dubbed in Uzbek language.

Uzbek artisans have been participating in the Surajkund Crafts Mela in Haryana. Indian music and dance groups always win several awards in the 'Sharq Taronalari' International Music Festival held in Samarkand every two years. [37] The cultural programs and food festivals organised by the Indian Embassy are extremely popular in Uzbekistan.

It is encouraging to note that the visits by the citizens of both the countries are also increasing. In 2017 a total of 14493 visas were

---

35 Embassy /High Commission /Consulate General of India. Accessed August 16, 2018. https://eoi.gov.in/tashkent/?2615?000.

36 Ibid

37 Ibid

granted to Uzbek nationals as compared to 13120 in 2016 and 11207 in 2015. In 2016 the number of tourist visas was 3380, business visas 1389 and medical visas 7676. The comparable figures for 2015 are 3253 tourist visas, 1186 business visas and 6215 medical visas. Since April 2017 Uzbek nationals are entitled to E-visas .Uzbekistan has also relaxed the procedure of issue of tourist visas to Indian nationals and this is likely to boost tourism from India to Uzbekistan.

The Way Ahead

In the last 28 years India and Uzbekistan have developed a deep sense of friendship, goodwill and co-operation. However, the lack of land connectivity has hampered the realisation of the full potential of trade and investments. Because of the continued instability in Afghanistan and the intransigence of Pakistan in not allowing trade with India through its territory, these obstacles are likely to continue to impede the full flowering of Indo-Uzbek relations.

India and Uzbekistan share civilisational values of tolerance and inclusion. Both the countries strongly believe in secular, democratic and constitutional polity and are keen to ensure peace and stability in Central Asia and Afghanistan. The two countries need to work together to align their perceptions and policies for future peace in Afghanistan so that they speak with the same voice in international fora like SCO. India needs to do more to explain its stand that the struggle against Taliban is both military and ideological. It may not be prudent for the concerned countries to accept a Taliban share in the governance of Afghanistan as it would inevitably lead to the dominance of Taliban over the entire territory of Afghanistan with serious consequences for its neighbors. To be a party in the national Government of Afghanistan the Taliban must shed their medieval philosophy, religious in-tolerance and anti-human rights convictions.

In the struggle against religious fundamentalism both India and Uzbekistan have strong convictions and a credible track record to combat extremism as well as terrorism. With India's joining of the SCO, this bilateral co-operation against terrorism would acquire a regional dimension also.

In sum, India and Uzbekistan have been reliable partners in promoting regional peace, stability and prosperity and are committed to continue working together both bilaterally and in the regional organisations.

Conclusion

Major General Rajiv Narayanan

The extant World Order is in a state of flux in this 'Age of Strategic Uncertainties', with the US in strategic retrenchment and the EU in an economic slowdown and internal dissonance. The recent events and trends show that the emerging World Order is tending towards multi-polarity leading to another period of jousting due to the 'balance of power'. This aspect is being felt closer home in the Af-Pak region that has seen this struggle for the geo-strategic and geo-political space in its full ferocity, ever since the Soviet Union overran Afghanistan in 1979. Over the last nearly four decades, while the players have morphed with some shifting their bias, the one constant has been the descent of Afghanistan into chaos.

This instability, sponsored by its neighbour and spurred by the other powers for regional dominance, has impeded the growth of the extended region. It has disrupted ancient linkages and connectivity and inhibited an integrated economic growth. The intransigence of Pakistan, in this regard, is worth mention. Blinded by its visceral hatred for India, for reasons best known to the Pakistan Army that drives its foreign policy, it has not only hurt the region but has also placed itself on the veritable edge of an internal economic collapse.

However, this geopolitical churning in the region brings with it the opportunity to evolve a new system of regional outreach for the present to transition to; an integrated approach that could work to provide stability, security and economic development in the region. In this regard the initiative taken by President Shavkat Mirziyoyev to reach out to the neighbouring countries augurs well for Central Asia as also for the extended neighbourhood. Concurrently the impetus under Prime Minister to 'Connect North' based on the 'Connect

Central Asia Policy' that was enunciated in 2012 complements the Uzbek initiative.

In this age of interdependence inter and intra-regional connectivity is essential for any economic growth. Under President Shavkat Mirziyoyev and Prime Minister Narender Modi this aspect has been given due impetus. Currently there are four transit routes that can be tapped for connecting South and Central Asia, bypassing the ancient route via Pakistan. These are, INSTC, Persian Gulf Corridor (Ashgabat Agreement), Chabahar (direct to Central Asia via Turkmenistan) and Chabahar (via Afghanistan). The last provides the shortest link to Uzbekistan and Central Asia. Towards this end India is developing the Shahid Beheshti Terminal in Chabahar, plans to extend a rail link from Chabahar to the Afghan border near Zabul and Uzbekistan is extending the rail link from Mazar – e – Sharif to Herat. This needs an extension to link it to Zabul, and the connectivity of Central Asia and Afghanistan to the global trade and India to Central Asia and Afghanistan would be complete.

The above would need stability and security in Afghanistan. Both India and Uzbekistan support an 'Afghan led and Afghan owned' peace process and prefers a regional response through extant institutions, like SCO and UN. The major threats identified are terrorism, religious extremism, trans-national crimes, drug trafficking and the support to the same from across its borders. There can be no military solution to the problem; however the need is to strengthen the military to enable it to provide security for the dialogue and political outreach to be successful. Both India and Uzbekistan need to work towards integrating Afghanistan into the global trade. The connectivity via Chabahar and the rail links being planned by India and Uzbekistan would facilitate this aspect. Education and empowerment of the youth, coupled with economic growth would invigorate the stability and security of Afghanistan. Concurrently the need is for providing health and medical services in each province of Afghanistan, could also be considered for the joint projects by India and Uzbekistan.

The initiative by President Shavkat Mirziyoyev for intra-regional connectivity, stability and good political relations and the geographical centrality of Uzbekistan in the region provides a very good opportunity to India for economic outreach with Uzbekistan and Central Asia. The fields of renewable energy, information and bio-technology, electrical equipment, defence industry, agro-food industry and creating supply value chain are some of the areas that could be considered for investment by Indian business houses. There is a need for the Central Asian nations to rework their extant economic policies to create a favourable environment for Indian investments, like repatriation of earnings, purchase costs, taxation, to name a few. The Free Economic Zones established by Uzbekistan could further the economic development of the region and Afghanistan.

Uzbekistan has had a very successful programme to counter the Islamic radicalisation of youth to ensure a demographic dividend to the country. Similarly, India has had a very different approach to the same problem primarily due to its syncretic society and cohesiveness of community and family structures. While Uzbekistan took a whole of government and society approach, India has successfully used the sociological and psychological approach that was assisted no end by the role models available in various spheres that the youth could look up to. Both can learn from each other's experiences and work towards ensuring that the demographic profile of both countries, and of the region, contributes as a dividend to the security, stability and economic development of the extended region.

India and Uzbekistan should work to strengthen the bilateral and multi-lateral arrangements, thereby enabling a consensus amongst regional and external players for a common approach to benefit the extended neighbourhood. The policy of the leaders of both countries provides an opportunity that can be grasped to counter the threats that have constantly engulfed this region. There are many 'Early Harvest Projects' that can be utilised to provide stimulus towards stability, security and economic development of Central and South Asia, including Afghanistan. It is for the decision makers to grasp the moment, as the strategic window maybe small in this geopolitical flux.

Contributors

Major General Rajiv Narayanan, AVSM, VSM (Retired) is a Distinguished Fellow, USI of India.

Rustam Khuramov is the head of Department, ISRS, under the President of the Republic of Uzbekistan.

Ambassador Asoke Kumar Mukerji was India's last Consul General to Soviet Central Asia from 1990-1991, and India's first resident Charge d'affaires in Uzbekistan, Tajikistan and Turkmenistan in 1992. He was Deputy Chief of Mission in India's Embassy to the Russian Federation between 2001-2005, Ambassador of India to Kazakhstan between 2005-2007, and Ambassador of India to the United Nations between 2013-2015.

Bakhtiyor Mustafayev is the Head of the Centre, ISRS under the President of the Republic of Uzbekistan.

Maj Gen BK Sharma, AVSM, SM** and Bar (Retd) is the Deputy Director (Research) and Head Centre for Strategic Studies and Simulation (CS3).

Rustam Makhmudov is a freelance expert. He has earlier worked at the ISRS under the President of the Republic of Uzbekistan, served in the Ministry of Foreign Affairs of the Republic of Uzbekistan.

Professor Nirmala Joshi is a Former Professor at the School of International Studies Jawaharlal Nehru University, New Delhi.

Timur Akhmedov is the head of the Department, ISRS under the President of the Republic of Uzbekistan.

Dr Adil Rasheed is Research Fellow at the Institute for Defence Studies and Analyses (IDSA), based in New Delhi.

Prof. Mirzokhid Rakhimov is the Director of Uzbekistan's contemporary history centre of Uzbekistan Academy of Science.

Ambassador S. R. Tayal was India's Ambassador to Uzbekistan. He was Ambassador of India to the Republic of Korea during 2008-11.

Index